Bitcoin for Beginners, Dummies & Idiots

By Giovanni Rigters

Table of Contents

Introduction

By now, you should have heard about cryptocurrency. There are different types of cryptocurrencies available, and they allow you to buy goods and services just like you do with fiat currency. You can also trade cryptocurrency for a profit. However, the concept of cryptocurrency is widely misunderstood by many people.

Cryptocurrency trading is highly lucrative, depending on how you handle your trade. Many individuals are skeptical of trading cryptocurrencies or using them to buy goods and services because of different myths and misconceptions surrounding them.

Many people ask the following questions concerning cryptocurrency. How can I buy cryptocurrency? Is cryptocurrency legal? Should I trade in cryptocurrency? How do I find reliable brokers that offer cryptocurrency? To get answers to these questions and other burning issues about cryptocurrency that you may want to know, this book is for you.

This book explains each cryptocurrency concept so you can learn more about it. It is divided into several chapters designed to help you gain full knowledge about cryptocurrencies and investing in them. It is possible to generate lucrative profits from cryptocurrency trading, but you should know how the system works to achieve your profit-oriented goals.

The first chapter provides basic details about what cryptocurrency is and how it functions. If you are a newbie in cryptocurrency trading, you need to understand the fundamentals of how different cryptocurrencies work.

There are different terms used in cryptocurrency trading, and these may seem to be complicated to understand. For instance, terms like blockchain technology, crypto mining, and others may seem intimidating at first.

However, once you go through this book, you will realize that these concepts help you make smarter trades. The trading strategy that you can choose is the same principle that you can apply to any type of online trade. Therefore, you should not be intimidated by unfamiliar terms and industry jargon, as you are going to realize in this book.

This book will also highlight different types of cryptocurrencies available that you can choose to trade. As you are going to see in this copy, cryptocurrency is also known as a digital currency, and it is intangible. In other words, you cannot store cryptocurrency in its physical state.

However, the concept you apply when trading foreign currency is just the same and applies to all types of trade. Before you begin trading cryptocurrency, you should choose the right one and understand its features. More than 10 000 cryptocurrencies are publicly traded on different platforms, so you have many to choose from.

You need to do your homework and choose the most appropriate cryptocurrency that you can trade. More cryptocurrencies continue to emerge, and they are increasing the total value of a digital currency. The other challenge that newbies often face concerning cryptocurrency trading relates to finding the ideal broker.

The ability to choose the ideal broker can go a long way in determining your quality of trade. In this book, you are going to learn many things about different trading platforms. You will read about the pros and cons of various crypto trading platforms and how they work.

Different methods are analyzed in this book about how you are going to choose the right broker. You will also learn various trends of cryptocurrency trading that you should analyze, like charts, basics of technical analysis, key levels, and moving averages. If you are wondering whether you should buy cryptocurrency or not, this book will explain everything that you want to know.

Generally, cryptocurrency trading is mainly speculative, and the markets are often volatile. You need to understand the risk associated with cryptocurrency so that you can make an informed decision. There is a chapter in this book that discusses in detail why you should invest in cryptocurrency and the risks that you are likely to encounter.

Buying and selling cryptocurrencies is a complicated area since it differs from the regular stock market. It takes time to understand how the often-volatile cryptocurrency market operates. The market volatility often scares away many traders.

This book will also highlight various trading strategies for beginners. For instance, short-term trading comes with specific time frames, and there is also long-term trading consisting of different trading strategies. Risk management is another critical component of cryptocurrency trading that you should know.

To keep your investment safe, you should do some research and try to be careful of elements like scamming and watch for red flags. Some returns are too good to believe, and the chances will be very high that they are scams.

If you fail to manage risk, it means that you are likely to suffer severe losses. This book provides comprehensive coverage of different topics related to cryptocurrency that every beginner needs to know.

Chapter 1: Basics of Cryptocurrency

The latest in investments is something that's not very clearly understood. While some people believe cryptocurrency to be the next gold rush, others believe it should not be spoken of. However, for people who are genuinely concerned about their investments and the way they invest their hard-earned money, it can be a herculean task to figure out what to do.

Once you understand the basics, it won't be very difficult for you to comprehend the scope of this technology that's promising to shake up the world. However, there is no dearth of these resources online, and trying to learn about cryptocurrency from the internet will only leave you more confused than before.

You can't even afford not to know about cryptocurrency because that'll mean losses for you. There's tremendous potential in the cryptocurrency trading market. If you fail to capitalize on it, you're not only missing out on making profits, but you're also losing money that could've been made.

So how do you learn about this bizarre new buzzword that everyone's talking about? You find a credible source that can summarize all the information for you in one place. This chapter will answer all your questions, clear up common misconceptions, and address your doubts about cryptocurrency so that you don't miss out on anything.

What Cryptocurrency Is

The simplest way to explain what cryptocurrency is that it's a decentralized currency. It can be used online to be exchanged for goods and services, just like the money you hold in your bank accounts. Being decentralized means that no bank or country can issue these cryptocurrencies, and even the processing or storage is out of the hands of these entities. The money you hold in your bank account can be withdrawn as cash, but cryptocurrencies have no physical form whatsoever.

Cryptocurrencies are just a set of data that are stored at multiple locations throughout the world. Almost all cryptocurrencies operate on the principle of blockchain technology, in which multiple computers all over the world are responsible for storing and maintaining records of transactions.

It almost works like a cloud technology which many people are more familiar with due to the increasing use of Google Drive, One Drive, Dropbox, and many other services.

The security in this technology is the utmost priority, and all the data is stored in an encoded form. Even if there's any sort of cyber-attack on one system, the others will still have the data intact. This also negates any possibility of fraud or currency counterfeiting since the records are maintained by many entities, and it's extremely difficult to cheat.

These are only some of the various benefits of cryptocurrency explained in a very basic manner. The scope and depth of cryptocurrency extend far beyond any other monetary system. In the further chapters, we'll be exploring all of these features in detail to enhance our understanding of the various cryptocurrencies.

Popular Cryptocurrencies

There are so many cryptocurrencies in the world that it's not possible to keep count. However, most novices don't realize this fact, and they assume it to be a nascent industry that revolves only around the all-powerful Bitcoin. There are more than 2,500 major cryptocurrencies, and that number's continuously growing, but it's to be noted that only a few of those are important and you need not know about every cryptocurrency out there.

Some of the most prominent cryptocurrencies that are traded all over the world are:

1. **Bitcoin:** The original cryptocurrency that everyone knows, Bitcoin was the first P2P e-cash system ever. It was used for the first time in 2010, and its value has crossed more than $32,000, which is an astounding figure. Bitcoin has been at the forefront of the cryptocurrency revolution, and the

products like Bitcoin SV and Bitcoin Cash have emerged in recent years.

2. **Ethereum:** The second-largest cryptocurrency in the world has shown a lot of promise, and it's expected to rise even more. The Ethereum blockchain is a vastly used platform all over the world. Ethereum doesn't only focus on the cryptocurrency side of things. It also focuses on the greater blockchain technology and its implementations.

3. **Dogecoin:** This cryptocurrency originated as nothing more than a joke, and its value has skyrocketed from what it used to be. The reason behind this astronomical gain is the social media hype generated in favor of doge. Even the owner of Tesla and SpaceX, Elon Musk, voiced his support for this cryptocurrency that further bolstered its position.

Types of Cryptocurrencies

You might think that there's only one type of cryptocurrency if you're not very well-versed with them. This isn't just a misconception among the unaware investors, but it's also a very common misconception among veteran investors. However, it's best to know about the different types of cryptocurrencies from an informational perspective. It'll help you identify which cryptocurrencies are the major players and which aren't. The two major types of cryptocurrencies are:

1. **Coins:** A coin-type cryptocurrency is what you must be familiar with, which is so for a good reason. The coins have their own blockchains, and whenever people talk about buying cryptocurrencies, it's usually this type that they're referring to. The most common cryptocurrencies of this type are Bitcoin, Ethereum, Ripple, and Litecoin.

2. **Tokens:** Now, this is where things get a little bit more complicated. The tokens are usually built on top of another pre-existing blockchain rather than having their own. The examples of tokens are numerous, but the most easily understandable would be dApp that runs on the Ethereum blockchain. Tokens are usually sold as an ICO (Initial Coin Offering) when they're first sold publicly, which is similar to the IPO (Initial Public Offering) in the stock market. Even these tokens are divided into two categories, namely the Utility Tokens and the Security Tokens. Discussing these tokens would take a very detailed discussion, and we wouldn't be discussing them here.

Reasons behind Popularity

Cryptocurrencies have risen to fame almost overnight. There are many theories as to why cryptocurrencies suddenly became so popular. However, just like all the theories, it's all just speculation, and there might be many other reasons at play as well.

The biggest reason for this immense popularity is that people know how scarce these cryptocurrencies are. Bitcoin will keep on halving in value after a few years, and the total amount of Bitcoin that can be mined is limited as well.

This is why people are rushing to get their hands on these cryptocurrencies as soon as they can. If people can get a hold of the cryptocurrencies sooner and at a lower value, they'll be able to sell them off for significant profits.

Another reason behind the popularity of cryptocurrencies is that there's zero interference from central banks and governments. The banks can't control the supply of these cryptocurrencies, and the inflationary pressures can be minimized due to this very reason. No one likes to be at the mercy of an institution run by a handful of people, and cryptocurrencies are paving the way for that very independence.

A small group of investors is also interested in cryptocurrency due to the technology behind it. These people are more curious than profit-minded, which is why they like to invest in cryptocurrencies. These people are staunch supporters of privacy and self-regulation, which is why they back blockchain-enabled cryptocurrencies. The security that's offered by blockchains is also very appealing since there are practically no risks involved like fraud and counterfeit currency.

Lastly, another huge reason behind the popularity of this technology is its short-term profitability. Since investors are always looking for new ways to make more money than before, the cryptocurrency market is a perfect place to double, triple, or even quadruple the initial investment.

These investments are usually not done for the long term due to the volatile nature of cryptocurrency. However, vigilant investors can easily increase their money in the short term.

Should You Be Investing in Cryptocurrencies?

Now that you know all the basics of cryptocurrency, the burning question on your mind must be if you should actually put your hard-earned money into something that's so new? The answer to this question can be a bit more complicated than a simple yes or no. This is because cryptocurrencies come with their own share of risks and benefits, just like any other investment. Many things can go wrong. Many things can go right.

Many veteran investors don't consider cryptocurrencies to be a stable and viable investment. They merely tag it as speculation that's bound to take a dip, a huge dip, for that matter. However, this isn't something that you can just brush off because it holds some truth. Cryptocurrencies differ from stocks in the sense that stocks generate money due to the company's increasing profits.

However, cryptocurrencies can't just generate profits inherently because they're only a digitized version of the same old currency. The only way you can make money with cryptocurrency is if someone has to pay more than you did, but if everyone decides to withdraw their funds, the cryptocurrency's value will take a plunge.

Even the great investment magnate Warren Buffet himself has said a few key things about the beloved Bitcoin. He compared it to a paper cheque because it can be used very efficiently to transfer money from one party to another - the advantage of cryptocurrency is its anonymity.

However, a cheque isn't worth any money if it's blank, and the same could be said about cryptocurrencies as well. Cryptocurrencies can be used to transmit money, but they can never have an intrinsic value of their own.

Another issue that plagues cryptocurrencies is stability. Even the much-touted Bitcoin has seen its fair share of fluctuations throughout its existence.

From 2017to 2020, the value of Bitcoin changed from $20,000 to a mere $3,200, and it should be a cause for concern. However, you can also argue that Bitcoin recovered its position and that it's still more profitable than the majority of stocks.

Nothing is without its flaws, and cryptocurrencies can't be expected to be flawless either. What should matter to you as an investor is the profits you can turn from an investment. If we go by the numbers, then the cryptocurrencies definitely paint a convincing picture. You have to be wise and cautious while investing in cryptocurrencies, but that goes for every other type of investment as well.

How to Invest

By now, you're aware of all the advantages and the possible pitfalls of cryptocurrencies. These points should make you feel confident in any decision you make. However, if you've decided to take the plunge and invest in lucrative cryptocurrencies, you should be wondering how to invest in them.

The most renowned cryptocurrencies like Bitcoin can easily be bought using US dollars. If you want to buy a lesser-known cryptocurrency that's just making its mark, you'll have to use a third-party wallet that requires you to make your purchases using Bitcoins or any other accepted cryptocurrency.

A wallet is essentially an online app that acts as a repository for all your cryptocurrency. You can create an account in under a few minutes, and that'll make you eligible to buy on the cryptocurrency exchange. This wallet can be used to both sell and buy these cryptocurrencies, and many of the online brokers who offer these wallets are now also offering their own cryptocurrencies.

If you want to balance out your investment portfolio, you should definitely look into cryptocurrencies, as they can help you establish a much more well-rounded profile.

Cryptocurrencies can offer you many benefits that aren't seen in the case of traditional bonds, mutual funds, and stocks. Unlike these traditional instruments, the cryptocurrency you buy is completely immune to any potential seizures or freezes by the local authorities of any nation.

Final Advice

It's all well and good if you want to invest in cryptocurrency, but there are a few key things you should keep in mind while doing so. Following these guidelines will help you protect yourself against any investments that might sink in the near future.

You should be especially careful while buying ICOs as they can be rather risky to dip your toes in. Try to find out as much as you can about the company that's offering this ICO, and you'll be able to determine the future prospects of your investment. You should know who owns the company and if they're reputed or not.

If you look at the other major investors putting their money into this ICO, you can safely go ahead as it increases the legitimacy of the cryptocurrency.

If a cryptocurrency is already established, then you'll be at a much lower risk of losing your money, but if the company is just raising money to develop it further, you're obviously at a higher risk. It all depends on the amount of risk you're willing to take, and the simple rule of "higher risks - higher profits" applies here as well.

It can be a long and challenging road to find the new prospects that hold the most promise, but this research is a part of the investing process itself. All the investors do their homework before they make the final bid or purchase, and you'll have to do the same as well.

Even if a cryptocurrency appears legitimate and full of promise, it doesn't necessarily mean that it'll be successful. You'll have to brace yourself for some losses, at least initially.

This book will discuss many of the concepts further in detail so that you can achieve greater clarity about cryptocurrencies. This introduction will provide you with a solid foundation to build upon, and you'll be able to grasp the associated concepts more easily. Remember that investing takes time and knowledge, you'll be equipped with proper knowledge in the further chapters, but time will have to be an investment that you make.

Chapter 2: Blockchain

You might have heard the term blockchain being used in regard to cryptocurrencies and how blockchain makes it possible for cryptocurrencies to be as secure as they are. However, more than just security, the blockchain technology itself has several features and traits which make it possible for cryptocurrency to exist and function the way it does.

This chapter will explore everything you need to know about blockchain technology and how this information will relate to cryptocurrencies.

History

While many people know that blockchain came into being in 2008 when Satoshi Nakamoto developed the design for a blockchain that would support digital currencies, the concept of blockchain already existed long before. In fact, it was in 1991 when Stuart Haber and Scott Stornetta developed the blockchain system.

However, back in 1991, it was very different from what it is today. There is no doubt that the modifications made by Nakamoto made it possible for blockchain to be such a perfect match for cryptocurrencies.

Though, it should be kept in mind that blockchain was not originally designed to work with cryptocurrencies. In the beginning, it was simply a database management system, which in many applications it still is, but the way that it manages data has evolved and improved quite drastically.

Purpose

At its core, blockchain technology is a database management system with a number of unique features, which makes it a very versatile technology. Due to its flexible nature, various security features, and unique types of functionality, it is a great basis for cryptocurrency and is also widely used in various other applications.

A digital database can be described as a system that electronically stores different types of data and information on a computer system. Moreover, databases use different sorting and classification criteria to organize the information to make it easy to access.

The main difference between a database and any other kind of data storage system is that a database allows multiple users to access information simultaneously while also giving them the ability to modify the information simultaneously. Moreover, databases allow people to store significantly larger amounts of data than other storage systems. The fact that this information is digitally stored means it can be accessed by people from any location as long as they can connect with the server.

Blockchain in Cryptocurrency

Generally, databases are owned by a person or business. The entity that owns the database also owns the server that the database exists on. One of the major differences between blockchain and other database systems becomes prominent, which is through a characteristic of blockchain known as Distributed Ledger Technology (DLT).

The blockchain is a database that stores transactions, much like a ledger used in accounting, though the way it stores this information makes it unique. This is where it is important to keep in mind the structure of a blockchain to better understand its capabilities in the context of cryptocurrencies.

As the name implies, a blockchain can be seen as a chain that consists of blocks. Information is grouped together and stored in a 'block.' Each block has a certain capacity, and once it has been filled with as much information as it can store, a new block is created to store more information.

This new block is added to the chain of existing blocks, creating a blockchain. Unlike other databases, in a blockchain, information is not stored in tables. Moreover, each block of information is created with a timestamp, and information on the block is stored chronologically.

Blockchain is known as a DLT because the entire blockchain doesn't exist on a computer or group of computers owned and operated by a single individual. Instead, the blockchains of cryptocurrencies rely on hosts known as nodes, which are computers or groups of computers owned and operated by different individuals or groups of people worldwide. This is great for the system's longevity and means that if one set of computers is damaged or fails, the blockchain still exists on other nodes.

Moreover, each node stores the entire blockchain, and it is a complete repository of all the information that the database holds, whereas computers in a traditional database each hold sections of the entire database. A few cryptocurrencies have a centralized storage system, though most rely on this DLT approach.

In the context of cryptocurrencies, the blockchain is a database that stores all the information about each transaction that occurs. Every trade of the cryptocurrency since the inception of the currency is recorded and stored on the blockchain, and users can verify every transaction.

Why DLT?

The distributed ledger technology holds many benefits for both the cryptocurrency and the users of the currency. While DLT has many benefits to blockchain in general and benefits many different operations that employ blockchain, to better understand the advantages of DLT, let's look at it in light of a cryptocurrency.

Decentralization

As a blockchain is hosted on several computer networks around the globe, it significantly reduces the risk of data being lost and the cryptocurrency being compromised even if one node is damaged or compromised.

Moreover, since each node has a complete record of the data, each node is important and can be used as a recovery point at any time. Since all transactions that happen on the currency are being updated to the nodes in real-time, there is no problem with nodes needing updates or syncing.

Secondly, if one node has an error or makes a mistake in recording a certain transaction, it has thousands of other nodes to reference to verify a transaction and correct its records. But more importantly, this eliminates the possibility of one node changing its own information deliberately.

If it were to do so, there would be a visible incoherence in the system as no other node will have that entry, making it obvious that something has been tampered with. Moreover, this process also serves as a strict security check since every transaction is verified with each node before being recorded by the blockchain, it becomes impossible to undo an entry. If one node says that an entry is incorrect and other nodes have already accepted it, it is not possible.

Had it been incorrect, it would not have passed the validation process, which required the approval of all other nodes. So not only can entries not be changed and altered, but they are also permanent and cannot be reversed either, making it a highly secure form of data storage.

While this works really well for currencies, it's also important to note that it is an extremely valuable tool for other sensitive information such as contracts, inventory information, individual ID information, and nearly any other kind of information.

If someone did decide to tamper with the information in a node and change some information stored on a specific block, they would need to access that block on every other node, or at least the majority of all other nodes. And, they would have to make that same change so that the majority of nodes would agree that the information change was correct, hence causing the remaining nodes to also change that information. However, considering the number of nodes and the fact that it is not easy to gain unauthorized access to a node, this is extremely unlikely.

Visibility

The fact that a cryptocurrency's blockchain is delegated to various nodes throughout the world has two main benefits in terms of the visibility of the system.

Firstly, those who have a personal node or have access to a node can actually see the transactions that are taking place in real-time. However, the general population can also use a blockchain explorer and get access to this same information. This increases the trust that people have in the system as they can see what is happening. And all this information is stored so they can even refer to it in the future.

Secondly, while the identities of the people making transactions are more difficult to decipher, it is much easier to see the value of transactions and the associated currency used to make this transaction. This makes it possible for a person to easily see the lifecycle and journey of one specific token on the cryptocurrency.

You can literally see where this token started off from and see all the transactions that it has been a part of. This is also an incredible security feature. If a token is stolen or an entire exchange is compromised, even though you can't see who is making a transaction, you can easily spot if someone is using stolen currency. This makes it very easy to keep the currency safe, as anyone who steals it will not be able to do much with it.

Security

While several features and functions of the blockchain do add security, there are other things that the blockchain does directly to enhance its security.

Blockchain technology employs a feature known as the 'hash.' When blocks are compiled in a blockchain, they follow a linear path. Each new block is placed 'above' the previous block, and in this manner, the blockchain grows in height. Every time a block is generated and added to the blockchain, it has its own unique hash as well as the hash of the block before it together with its timestamp.

Generating the hash is a complex process as the hash is a mathematical function of the information within the block represented in the form of an alphanumeric code. Therefore, if the information contained within the block is altered, the correlated hash code also changes.

This effect carries on to the next block as well. In this way, a small change in the information in one block leaves a visible effect on the hash code, which becomes an inconsistency that is easy to spot.

Therefore, if someone wanted to beat the system successfully, not only would they have to alter the information in that block in the majority of the nodes that exist, even if they chose just to alter the information on their own node, they would still need access to a lot of other nodes for that change to be accepted and implemented across the blockchain.

While this may seem possible in a very small blockchain, considering this approach for a large, well-established cryptocurrency is not feasible. There are hundreds of thousands of nodes even in the smaller mainstream cryptocurrencies, and the amount of money it would cost together with the amount of expertise that would be needed simply isn't possible. Moreover, even if it were possible, with so many people watching the cryptocurrency, people would easily detect this unusual activity and identify it as an attack. If somehow the attack was successful, node owners would simply abandon that block and take a fresh start from the previous unaffected blocks, making this entire endeavor useless.

Blockchain at Large

Blockchain has a lot of functionality outside of the cryptocurrency realm. In fact, cryptocurrency has nearly acted as a catalyst to market the power of blockchain as a system, and people from all walks of life understand how they can make use of blockchain in their trade.

Blockchain has been especially useful in the financial services market, particularly in the asset management area. Prior to blockchain, systems were slow, prone to error, and rather labor-intensive. Moreover, the entire process for specific activities such as asset management required a lot of people to keep track of what was going on, on their own accord.

Everyone from the broker to the custodian to the end client was responsible for documenting the process and keeping a copy for reference. The entire process has become far less risky through blockchain, much more transparent for everyone involved, and very easy to do as everyone can collaborate on one shared platform.

Similarly, those that work in insurance claim also have to go through a lot of paperwork, and they have to sift through a lot of files which are already quite weak to begin with. There is a high risk of fraudulent claims, expired policies, and poorly gathered data, considering that this is all done manually.

Not only is it labor-intensive, but there is also a strong possibility of error. Through the blockchain mechanism, all of these things can be streamlined, and the encryption tool of the platform allows for excellent security.

While there are many solutions for global payment, many of these systems are not very efficient. Even though there are banks and proper global payment platforms, getting money to a different country can be a lengthy process. Moreover, the institutions that facilitate this process often charge a high fee, take several days to process, and there is no way to stop money laundering.

The blockchain platform has proven to be very effective in the remittance market, and many of the existing global payment service providers are incorporating blockchain technology to enhance their services. On the other hand, several new companies rely solely on the blockchain mechanism and use this platform as their unique feature to attract clients. Through the blockchain system, global payments are not only done instantly, but they are far more secure for everyone involved. The sender, the receiver, and the intermediary know exactly what is going on.

For governments, this has proven to be a magical instrument as it allowed them to have more control over how money flows in and out of their country. However, as there are still a lot of remittance services that rely on traditional systems, money laundering is still not completely under control, but it seems far more possible to manage this problem.

Difficulties with Blockchain

While it is a wonderful system with many benefits for many professions, it still does have its fair share of drawbacks.

Something less known about blockchain is its extremely high fuel requirements. It is a digital system that runs on electricity, but it requires an incredible amount of power to run, and creating electricity is not very environmentally friendly.

Some of the top cryptocurrencies using blockchain consume more electricity than entire countries do. In fact, they use more electricity than what would be used by dozens of countries put together.

On the other hand, while the complexity of the blockchain is what we are benefitting from, it is also something that hinders this technology. It is complex, making it difficult for people to understand how it works, and eventually making them less likely to use it. And it also makes it a very difficult market to enter since people don't know enough about it to actually benefit from it by incorporating it into their businesses and daily lives. While it is a simple system, in theory, applying it to a certain problem in a certain industry is a challenging task.

Chapter 3: Cryptocurrency Mining

Cryptocurrency mining is a critical component that helps in the development and maintenance of the blockchain ledger. It also involves the process of the creation of cryptocurrency and how it is introduced in circulation. Different things are involved in crypto mining which has been popular with miners, cybercriminals, and investors. This chapter discusses in detail the concept of cryptocurrency mining and how it works.

What Is Crypto Mining?

Crypto mining is a process that involves the verification of transactions between different users. The data blocks are validated, which helps add transaction records to the blockchain public ledger, which is also known as a public record. The process of crypto mining also involves the creation of new cryptocurrencies through the process of solving puzzles or cryptographic equations using computers.

The introduction of new coins in the supply circulation is one of the key factors that allow different cryptocurrencies to work as a decentralized network. As a result, cryptocurrencies do not require the central authority of a third party like fiat currency. The central bank regulates fiat currency in any country.

Crypto mining plays a pivotal role in maintaining all ledger transactions to ensure that they are verified easily. The miners use complex machinery to solve math problems within the crypto network. The mining operation produces new crypto, and bitcoin is one of the most popular cryptocurrencies.

The miners also make the crypto payment network secure and trustworthy by solving computational problems. Mining also helps in verifying all transaction information.

How Does Cryptocurrency Mining Work

If you are interested in cryptocurrency mining, you should know that the exercise is rewarding. Many investors consider crypto mining because the miners are handsomely rewarded with crypto tokens for their great work. However, before you invest in cryptocurrency mining, there are different things that you should know about how the concept works.

A miner is viewed as a node in a network that plays a role in collecting transactions and organizing them into blocks. The network nodes or miners will receive information about all transactions made, and they are responsible for verifying their validity. The miner nodes will begin to gather these transactions from a memory pool and assemble them into a block.

The first stage in mining a block involves hashing every transaction that is obtained from a memory pool. The miner node will add a transaction where he awards himself a block reward or mining reward before they begin the mining process. The transaction involving a block reward is known as the coin-base, and this is where cryptos or coins are created from nowhere.

This usually involves the first transaction that is recorded in the new block. When each transaction has been hashed, we get what is called hashes, organized into a hash tree or Merkel tree. This tree comes from organizing different transactions into pairs that are hashed together. You repeat the process of pairing the outputs and hashing them until you reach the top of the tree (a hash tree).

The top part of this tree is known as Merkle root or root hash. The top hash appears as a single hash that will represent the previous hashes used to build it.

Together with the hash belonging to the previous block, the root hash and a random number known as a nonce are put into the block's header. This block header is again hashed to produce an output consisting of the previous elements that include root hash, nonce, and the previous block's hash together with other elements. The block hash is the output, and it will play a role as the identifier of the new block created (candidate block).

The block hash or output must be less than a specific target value that is usually decided by the protocol for it to be regarded as valid. The block should begin with a particular number of zeros. This target value is also called the hashing difficulty, and the protocol regularly adjusts it while ensuring that the rate of new blocks being developed remains proportional to the level of hashing power constant to the network.

As a result, whenever new miners are joining the network, competition will increase, thereby raising the hashing difficulty. The average block time is prevented from decreasing. In contrast, the hashing difficulty goes down when the miners choose to leave the network. The block time is maintained at a constant level, although there will be less computational power that is dedicated to any network.

The mining process compels the miners to continue hashing the block header repeatedly through the nonce until the time when one miner in the network ultimately provides a valid block has. The attainment of a valid has means that the founder node then broadcasts the block on the network. This hash is verified and validated by all other nodes. After validating the block, they add it into their blockchain then move to the next stage of mining another block.

If two miners simultaneously broadcast a valid block, the result is that the network may end up having two competing blocks. The miners will use the block first received to start mining the next block. In the meantime, the two blocks continue to compete until the time when the next block is mined. One of the blocks will be abandoned in the process, and it is called the stale block or orphan block. Eventually, the miners of the block then switch back to the process of mining the winning block's chain.

In brief, crypto miners play a pivotal role in verifying the legitimacy of transactions to get rewards for their work. The rewards come in the form of cryptocurrency that helps to create a new currency. You need to understand how blockchain works to gain a full understanding of cryptocurrency mining. The following are the key takeaways of cryptocurrency mining:

- Through mining, you earn cryptocurrency without investing any money.
- Miners earn cryptocurrency for completing verified transactions or blocks that are added to the blockchain.
- A miner who discovers the solution to a complex puzzle wins the rewards. The mining power in the network determines your probability of discovering a solution to complex hashing puzzles.

To solve complex puzzles, you will need an application-specific integrated circuit (ASIC) or graphics processing unit to help you set up a mining rig. The following section outlines the technology you will need to succeed in crypto mining.

Mining Hardware

If you want to build a system that you can use for mining cryptocurrency, you need to get powerful hardware to get started. First and foremost, you must acquire a mining rig or a customized PC that consists of common elements, including RAM, motherboard, CPU, and storage.

However, the graphics cards required significantly differ as a result of the hard work involved in cryptocurrency mining. You will need a powerful GPU, and the chances of buying more than one will be very high. You will need to connect more graphics cards to the motherboard, and you also need more power supply to operate the system.

You also need a motherboard that is capable of accommodating more graphics cards. Other motherboards can accommodate up to 19 graphics cards, but they require a specific layout that you should follow. You also need the Intel Core i5 CPU, and you do not necessarily need to overspend on this one since it works perfectly well with the ideal motherboard.

Other forms of hardware that you will need include RAM, PSU, storage, PCI-e Riser, Nvidia graphics card, and AMD graphics card. On top of the hardware, you also need to get an appropriate power supply to operate the hardware.

In other words, you should get insight into the kind of equipment required to mine cryptocurrency successfully. If you are interested in mining competitively, you must invest in high quality and powerful computer equipment that include GPU or application-specific integrated circuit (ASIC). These components can cost you thousands of dollars. You need to get a fast-mining rig, or else you may consider joining a mining pool, as you will see below.

Mining Software

Cryptocurrency mining involves the use of sophisticated computers to solve computational math problems that are extremely complex. As a result, you need to get the appropriate software after getting your hardware. Choosing the right program for your computer will help to connect you to the blockchain network. Essentially, mining software is designed to deliver work to the miners, collect results for the work done, and add the information to the blockchain.

The other purpose of crypto mining software is to monitor all the miners' activities. It shows crucial statistics like cooling, temperature, average mining speed, and hash rate.

There are also free programs that you can consider to mine cryptocurrency like Bitcoins. Some of these programs can run on different operating systems, but they also come with advantages and disadvantages that you must know. Mining pools, in particular, provide their software to the miners. Mining software can be customized to suit the needs of the miners.

Software like Nice Hash Miner is good for beginners since it is easy to use, and it can mine several cryptocurrencies. The software automatically chooses the best algorithm that is profitable.

All you need to do is download the software and install it on the device that you would like to use for mining. The advantage of crypto mining software is that it helps to secure the decentralized digital currency.

Crypto mining software also helps you to earn cryptocurrency without investing any money. Additionally, you should also know that cryptocurrency works well in conjunction with mining hardware. In other words, the software helps you connect your mining pool with the hardware. When choosing mining software, make sure that it is user-friendly.

Mining Pools

The block usually grants the miner who solves the problem or first discovers the hash a reward, but the probability of getting the hash constitutes the combined mining power of the entire network. If a miner has a small portion of mining power, they stand a small opportunity of finding the next block. As a result, mining pools are specifically created to help solve this challenge. As the name suggests, pooling involves a process of combining computational resources by the miners who all share the power to process different activities over a network. This will help to ensure that the reward is split equally among every participant in the pool.

The reward is allocated according to one's amount of work they contribute to improving the probability of getting the block. If you are interested in making a profit through cryptocurrency mining, you have a choice of joining a mining pool where all the miners combine their devices to increase hashing output or go solo. There are different methods of mining pools, and they do not operate the same way.

Proportional pooling is the most common method, and the miners receive shares according to the pool's success in finding the block. Later on, the miners get rewards that are proportional to the shares they hold. Pay-per-share is another pooling method that gives miners shares according to their contributions. The miners get instant payouts. The other method is peer-to-peer pool mining that aims to prevent the centralization of the pool structure.

The primary benefit of a mining pool is that it promotes teamwork which increases the chances of success. While you can go solo where you get full ownership of the reward, chances of succeeding are slim because of the requirements of the resources. Mining cryptocurrency is costly since it requires costly hardware and high electricity costs. However, when you are operating as a team, you will use fewer resources in terms of electricity and hardware, which improves the success rate.

Mineable Cryptocurrency

Bitcoin is probably the most popular form of cryptocurrency to date. The concept of cryptocurrency mining started with Bitcoin in 2009, and it has since gained widespread acceptance in other cryptos. For greater rewards, small miners must work with big pools for better rewards. Not all cryptocurrencies can be mined as a result of several reasons.

There are more than 10,000 cryptocurrencies available, and the mineable ones use Application Specific Integrated Circuit (ASIC) that is designed to mine certain crypto assets. If you do not upgrade your ASIC miner, it can be difficult for you to compete with other miners actively.

To choose the crypto to mine, you must first check the exchanges that support the coin. Coins supported by less popular exchanges can be difficult to withdraw since you can only do it to the internal wallet. You must know if it is possible to withdraw your cryptocurrency to fiat.

The miner can end up paying heavy commissions for withdrawals. You also need to ensure that cryptocurrency mining is legal in your country, as explained in detail below. Before you buy the mining equipment, you must evaluate its long-term use. You must go through different reviews to get insight into the mineable cryptocurrencies.

Is Cryptocurrency Mining Legal?

You need to question the legality of cryptocurrency mining to be on the safe side. Your geographic location determines whether crypto mining is legal or not. The concept of cryptocurrency can undermine the dominance of government control of fiat currencies in the financial markets. As you are now aware, cryptocurrency is not controlled by a central bank like fiat currency.

In other places like China, Pakistan, Egypt, Morocco, Bolivia, Nepal, Algeria, and Ecuador, cryptocurrency mining and ownership are illegal. However, cryptocurrency use is increasingly becoming legal across different parts of the globe.

You also need to understand the risks of crypto mining which often come as financial and regulatory. Crypto mining is generally a financial risk, as highlighted above. After spending thousands investing in mining equipment, you may only realize later that the return on investment is nil. In other countries, there are sets of regulations that prohibit the practice of crypto mining. Therefore, you need to research the countries where cryptocurrency mining is legal before you get into it.

In brief, crypto mining refers to the process of working complex computational puzzles to earn cryptocurrency as a reward for the finished work. People usually mine crypto to get an additional source of income. Mining cryptocurrency involves the process of verifying all the transactions between different users. After validating the transactions, they are added to the blockchain public record. In other words, the entire process of crypto mining involves the creation of cryptocurrencies through solving complex problems with a computer.

There are also other reasons why you can consider cryptocurrency mining or trading. Some people turn to cryptocurrency trading because it is flexible, and it gives them financial freedom. Unlike fiat currency that is centralized and controlled by a central government, cryptocurrency is decentralized. The area of cryptocurrency mining is significantly gaining popularity with many investors. However, it is also attracting cybercriminals who are bent on trying their luck.

Chapter 4: Types of Cryptocurrencies

As of January 2021, there were over 4,000 listed cryptocurrencies in existence. Although many of them have very zero to little trading volume, others are highly popular among e-commerce communities, other devoted communities, and many investors. Did you know that just three years ago, during 2018, there were just 1583 listed cryptocurrencies on coinmarketcap.com and that there are currently only 180 fiat currencies in the world?

You are probably wondering why there are so many cryptocurrencies and what sets them apart from one another. Just 12 years ago, in 2009, Bitcoin was the only cryptocurrency there is. Today, we have cryptocurrencies, more or less, designated for each sector of the economy.

All of these cryptocurrencies virtually have the same goal. This goal is leveraging blockchain technology to restructure fields such as finance, energy, health, data storage, security, privacy, payments, machine learning, social networking, content ownership, logistics and supply, and other areas of equally high diversity. You may be thinking that so many cryptocurrencies already exist, so what exactly is the main reason behind their expansive growth and proliferation?

The reason is quite simple: each cryptocurrency serves a different purpose and has distinct functionalities. Typically, the primary blockchain is perhaps why we have so many different cryptocurrencies. It basically gives developers the scope needed to create several cryptocurrencies to tackle different functionalities.

It goes without saying that there are cryptocurrencies that serve the purpose of a "normal" currency. Like regular fiat ones, these currencies have a set value that can be essentially used to make purchases or for trade in general. The popular Bitcoin falls under this cryptocurrency umbrella. Other cryptocurrencies, however, may fall under the function of utility. This means that there are groups of cryptocurrencies that are developed as an infrastructure.

This means that they allow for other cryptocurrencies to be forged on top of their own networks. For instance, Ethereum, which we will be discussing in more depth throughout this chapter, and Ethereum Virtual Machine, fall under this category. Ethereum, with its latter blockchain-based software platform, allows several token coins to be created on its network.

The other major types of cryptocurrencies, which are referred to as platform or app cryptocurrencies, are made to be built on top of other utility currencies. One great example of this type of cryptocurrency is the

Augur cryptocurrency that was established on the Ethereum network.

This, in short, explains the need for, or rather the reason behind the existence of, many different cryptocurrencies. Keep in mind that blockchain technology is not really under anyone's control. Simply put, anyone who is knowledgeable enough about the inner workings of the technology can make their own cryptocurrency. If you look back at how this whole virtual technology phenomenon started out, the first one to use blockchain technology was Satoshi Nakamoto.

He came up with Bitcoin and was the first one to implement this understanding into something this revolutionary. It wasn't long after that other developers realized that they might be able to expand on Nakamoto's idea, exploiting this technology to create more innovative and perhaps "better versions" of Bitcoin. One of the first altcoin creators, Charlie Lee, who was also a former Google engineer, played a great role in the creation of Litecoin. This was when many others joined the quest to create something even larger than Bitcoin.

One other reason why there are this many cryptocurrencies in the world may be due to the fact that Bitcoin, among a few other altcoins, has witnessed a great deal of success. When Bitcoin first came out, many people referred to it as the "monkey business." Not many people understood it, and others thought it would be a scam in the long run. It was, to a great extent, highly disregarded. Bitcoin, at the time, had no value. Because it didn't seem promising, very few people actually thought to understand it. However, it proved to show immense success and value over the years.

Similarly, Ethereum was practically worthless up until the beginning of 2017. It was during 2017 that Bitcoin and the other altcoins thrived. It was when Bitcoin's value rose to $20,000 per BTC. It was also when many people started to turn their heads to the world of cryptocurrency. In this chapter, we will explore the most popular cryptocurrencies in more depth.

Bitcoin

Bitcoin is a decentralized digital currency that can be sold, bought, and directly exchanged. You don't need an intermediary or a bank to handle your Bitcoins. There is a public ledger that anyone can access to view every Bitcoin transaction ever made. This ledger makes transactions hard to fake or reverse. The value of Bitcoins is purely determined by its system, meaning that no issuing institution or government is backing the currency.

Bitcoin is built on blockchain, which has already been covered extensively in the previous chapters. Many people think of Bitcoin as an alternative investment or a way to diversify one's portfolio beyond bonds and stocks. While it can be used to make purchases, not many vendors accept Bitcoin as a means of payment.

Some services also allow you to connect your crypto account to your personal debit card. You can buy Bitcoins via exchanges, which work almost similarly to brokerage accounts.

You will need a digital wallet, either hot or cold, to store your coins. Hot or online wallets are ones where you store your coins in the cloud through a provider or exchange. A cold or mobile wallet allows you to store your coins on an offline device. You can invest in Bitcoins through special retirement accounts or Bitcoin mutual funds.

Ethereum

Like every other cryptocurrency, Ethereum is a decentralized currency that is built on the principles of a blockchain network. Everyone in the Ethereum network gets a copy of a ledger that allows them to see all transactions. Like Bitcoin, Ethereum can be bought, sold, and used to make purchases. Many people invest in Ethereum because of its rapid success and rapidly increasing value.

Ethereum, however, is different in the sense that it allows users to create applications that can be run on the blockchain. This is similar to how software runs on a computer. These applications can be designed to deal with intricate financial transactions and transfer and store personal data. Ethereum is unique because it can perform various functions. Other than being a currency and its ability to handle financial transactions, Ethereum can be used to perform smart contracts. Third-party users may also use it to store data. It is also characterized by its constant innovation, huge, already existing network, and lack of intermediaries.

Its only disadvantages may be that it has a high inflation potential, its transaction costs are soaring, it is difficult for developers to pick up, and it holds a rather uncertain future. To buy Ethereum, you can choose a cryptocurrency exchange, deposit actual fiat money, or buy Ether along with other assets at the current Ethereum price. You can use a different wallet to store your coins instead of using your trading platform's standard digital wallet, as using it can be a security risk.

Binance Coin

Binance exchange and trade is a platform that issued Binance Coin. This cryptocurrency, with the BNB symbol, started out on the Ethereum blockchain. However, it is now a separate entity of the Binance chain. One-fifth of Binance's profits are designated to the permanent burning of the Binance Coins in its treasury each year. It was initially created to serve as a discounted trading fees utility token in 2017.

However, it has since grown to encompass various other applications, like travel bookings, transaction fee payments, entertainment, financial services, and many other online services. According to a Bloomberg report, the Justice Department and Internal Revenue

Service are currently investigating Binance coin as of May 13, 2021.

Tether

Tether, which trades as USDT, was previously known as Realcoin and was established by Tether Operations Limited in 2014. This entity was created by Bitfinex, which is a Hong Kong-based cryptocurrency exchange. Tether is designed to function as a stablecoin or a cryptocurrency that is attached to real-time commodities or assets.

Its function is to help guarantee value stability and eliminate market volatility, which is why investors use it. Because it serves to safeguard financial stability in case the crypto market ultimately crashes, Tether is at an advantage over Ethereum and Bitcoin. Similarly, Tether can be attached to fiat currencies, like the USD, Swiss Franc, Euro, metals, and other precious commodities.

Tether claims that it circulates the cryptocurrency market at a 1:1 ratio with the USD. You can buy Tether at a global exchange program. While Tether is the first-ever stablecoin, it seems to fail to live up to its claims. Many people question the extent of this stablecoin's legitimacy and whether the number of USDs in its reserves matches the number of Tether in circulation. Other people believe that Tether was never an actual cryptocurrency and that its creation was an attempt to manipulate Bitcoin's market position and value. Moreover, the cryptocurrency experienced trouble with US financial regulators and banks. These troubles ranged from insufficient documentation loss cover-up to embezzlement.

Cardano

Cardano, which is a third-generation decentralized cryptocurrency, is designed to be a more efficient alternative to the proof-of-work networks. This is because it is designed on a proof-of-stake blockchain platform.

This blockchain platform allows people to validate or block transactions according to the number of coins that they hold. Proof-of-work networks, like Ethereum, are characterized by their sustainability, scalability, and interoperability, and it has become exceptionally hard to deal with their increased energy use, growing costs, and sluggish transaction times.

Charles Hoskinson, Ethereum's co-founder, in turn, understood the complications that came along with the proof-of-work networks and decided to work on Cardano to provide plausible solutions to these challenges. Cardano, in its foundation stages, created the Ouroboros consensus protocol, which it uses to run. Ouroboros is the first consensus protocol that proves to be secure and is extensively supported by academic research.

The first Cardano product resumed being advertised as an identity management tool that allows access to various services. For instance, eligibility for government aid and credentials needed to open a bank account can both be verified using Cardano. The two other products that Cardano markets use a supply chain to trace the journey of products. A smart contract platform, similar to Ethereum, is also being developed by Cardano. This smart contract platform can be used to develop decentralized apps on an enterprise level.

Project Catalyst, a democratic on-chain governance system, will also be used by Cardano's team to manage the execution of various projects. You can buy Cardano by Opening an online exchange account and purchasing an optional wallet for security purposes.

Polkadot

Polkadot is also a third-generation blockchain protocol that is designed to connect several specialized blockchains into a united network. Polkadot is created to serve as a portion of a great vision, which is essentially a web where users are back in control over the different internet monopolies. It is built on the foundations of other blockchain networks.

However, it still offers other substantial benefits. Since Polkadot is a sharded multichain network, it is able to process numerous transactions that occur on different chains simultaneously, unlike other blockchains in isolation that can process only a limited or specific amount of traffic. This means that Polkadot can get rid of the bottlenecks that other legacy networks may have experienced. This gives this cryptocurrency the advantage of being highly scalable, as it allows it to adopt the right environment needed to grow in the future.

Parachains are the sharded chains that are associated with Polkadot. This name references the ability to run parallelly on the network. With blockchain networks, there is no such thing as a mold. There are, however, trade-offs. This means that each cryptocurrency has to give up something in return for a specific feature or function. While one chain may serve as an identity management system, another may be great at file storage.

When it comes to Polkadot, there are various blockchains with innovative designs that are perfected for a certain use. This means that you have optimal effectiveness, efficiency, services, and security. Because it uses a Substrate development framework, each team's blockchain can be customized and developed rapidly and efficiently. You can share functionalities and data on Polkadot applications and networks, just like you would on your phone. This entails that you don't have to resort to centralized service providers for additional costs.

This is because Polkadot provides cross-chain communication and interoperability, making it ideal for the development of creative services and the transferring of information across chains. On Polkadot, you are allowed to govern your networks however you like. Generally speaking, there is a see-through stake in Polkadot's entire network governance. You can customize these networks on your blockchain to suit your needs, which would allow you to experiment and switch out ready-made modules. You can easily upgrade and tweak your models as you go.

Ripple

Ripple, a currency exchange network and payments settlement system, supports global transactions. Ripple functions as a trusted agent or intermediary between two different entities throughout a transaction. This network can help you determine whether your transaction or exchange has seamlessly gone through. It can help make exchanges between various fiat currencies, cryptocurrencies, and other commodities, like gold and silver, a much easier process.

When you make a transaction using Ripple, it deducts a rather small amount of XRP, which is a cryptocurrency that runs on the XRP ledger. 0.00001 XRP is the standard transaction fee on Ripple. Besides functioning as a means to facilitate transactions, XRP can be used as an investment. Ripple is characterized by its fast settlement and transaction confirmation, very low fees, versatile exchange network that encompasses fiat currencies, cryptocurrencies, and commodities, and the fact that huge entities use it.

The disadvantage of using Ripple may be that it is rather centralized and has a large pre-mined XRP supply. It should also be noted that the SEC filed a lawsuit against Ripple in 2020.

Litecoin

Litecoin is a peer-to-peer, decentralized virtual currency. With Litecoin, you can make almost no-cost, instant payments. These transactions can be made globally, by institutions or sole individuals. This cryptocurrency, like Ethereum and Bitcoin, uses the proof-of-work algorithm to secure its network.

As we hinted above, this algorithm required a party to prove to the other involved parties in the same network that a certain transactional amount has been expended. Litecoin can be used as a method of paying other parties located anywhere on Earth. It doesn't require you to resort to an intermediary to have your transaction processed.

Chainlink

Chainlink is an oracle network that donates real-time data to the blockchain's smart contracts. Like other cryptocurrencies, Chainlink is decentralized. As you can infer from the name, the digital asset token that's used to pay for the network's services is called "LINK." The good thing about the currency is that its verifiable and immutable smart contracts are automatically executed in the framework constructed in an IF/Then structure whenever the conditions are met. Additionally, oracles on blockchain networks can bring off-chain information to on-chain smart networks. However, since oracles may be faulty, they may counteract the benefits of on-chain smart networks.

Stellar

Stellar has many similarities to Ripple. For one, it is a payment technology whose goal is to bring financial institutions together and eliminate the time and costs of cross-border transfers. Both networks have also initially used the same protocol. A decentralized server network is run along with a distributed ledger.

This ledger is typically updated every 2 to 5 seconds on every node. What sets Stellar and Bitcoin apart is Stellar's consensus protocol. This protocol doesn't require the whole miner network to approve transactions and uses the Federated Byzantine Agreement algorithm in its place.

Innovation is also a great driving factor behind the abundance of cryptocurrencies. We humans, by nature, are innovation-driven. We are constantly in search of improvement, and similarly, cryptocurrencies are too. While many cryptocurrencies may essentially handle similar issues, they still differ in the protocol, tweaking various elements. For example, many platforms may promise a life-changing smart contracts platform. While Ethereum still remains the leading smart contracts platform, others are trying to catch up with its success in that area. If you read this chapter, then you now understand how each cryptocurrency has different services to offer.

Chapter 5: Cryptocurrency Wallets

Are you new to cryptocurrency trading? What do you need to make cryptocurrency transactions? Have you heard about cryptocurrency wallets? How do they work? If you're just beginning in cryptocurrency trading, there are a few things you need to be aware of. To buy or sell cryptocurrencies, you will need to have a cryptocurrency wallet. However, a cryptocurrency wallet does not store your money as your pocket wallet does. A cryptocurrency does not exist in physical form at all.

Unlike traditional wallets, a cryptocurrency wallet is a digital tool to help you track records of the transactions stored on the blockchain. To start investing in cryptocurrency, you will be required to have a safe wallet that can store your private and public keys. These keys are essentially codes that help you make a transaction through blockchain technology. This chapter will look at what a cryptocurrency wallet is and the different types of wallets you can choose from. In addition to this, you will learn the best methods to choose a wallet for your cryptocurrency transactions.

What Is a Cryptocurrency Wallet?

A software, device, program, physical medium, or service that helps you store your private and public keys necessary to carry out cryptocurrency transactions, is known as a wallet. A secure wallet is necessary to store the essential keys. In addition to this, cryptocurrency wallets offer encryption for your data. With that said, a cryptocurrency wallet often offers to sign information that can be used to execute a transaction, identify a document, or for legal signatures.

In simple words, cryptocurrency wallets can be understood as programs that act as an interface for users to monitor their transactions, transfer money, and carry out other operations. Essentially, when a person transfers any cryptocurrency to you, they are, in essence, transferring the ownership of it to your wallet's address, also known as your public address.

This is where your private keys play an important role. You will only be able to access the transferred digital currency in your wallet if the combination of your public and private keys is found to be authentic.

When the wallet's address to which the cryptocurrency has been transferred matches the private key of the user, the amount is deducted from the sender account and subsequently increased in the recipient's wallet. However, being a cryptocurrency trader, it is essential to remember that transactions from wallet to wallet do not mean the actual exchange of physical money. The cryptocurrency wallet will essentially signify and display the record of the transactions on the blockchain. In addition to this, the wallet is responsible for showing you the change in your balance of cryptocurrencies.

Types of Cryptocurrency Wallets

There are not one but many types of cryptocurrency wallets available at your disposal. Depending on your needs and the way you plan to use your wallet, you can select the best wallet for yourself based on the different features provided by the different types of wallets. In addition to the basic features, the various types of cryptocurrency wallets allow you to access your cryptocurrency account in different ways. In this section, we will discuss the different types of cryptocurrency wallets and their characteristics.

Paper Wallets

For people who want to keep their cryptocurrency transactions and private keys offline, paper wallets can help them store their information securely. Although paper wallets are not very relevant anymore, they are the second most secure method to store the information related to cryptocurrency transactions. When the very first cryptocurrencies were launched, paper wallets provided the sole and secure way to store important information. Since paper wallets require immense technical knowledge, very few people initially bought and stored digital currencies.

In addition to this, the people who used paper wallets to store crypto assets had to be very cautious. Even minor discrepancies could lead to expensive problems. However, with advances in technological systems and digital platforms, better and more effective types of wallets emerged.

In paper wallets, a user prints their public and private keys on a piece of paper to start transacting digital currencies. Since the confidential information about the private keys and public addresses of users is stored offline on paper, this type of wallet is a secure way to store information about crypto assets. While not all cryptocurrencies offer the option of paper wallets, many of the old and popular digital currencies still offer their users a chance to use paper wallets. However, it is vital to be cautious while using paper wallets.

Paper wallets are easy and secure to use. While a paper wallet can simply refer to a printout of your crypto assets and other information, the term can also refer to a program that is used to generate your public and private keys securely and print them on paper. If you wish to transfer cryptocurrency, you can transfer the required amount from your software wallet to the public key printed on your paper wallet.

Similarly, you can transact the cryptocurrency from your paper wallet to your software wallet when you want to withdraw funds. The process of manually scanning the QR code on your paper wallet is also known as sweeping. With that said, as cryptocurrencies gained popularity and started being adopted widely, people started using other types of cryptocurrency wallets.

Online Wallets

This type of wallet allows the user to access the cryptocurrency portfolio through any device that is connected to the Internet. Although they are not as secure as paper wallets, online wallets have good usability. The information about your crypto assets, public address, and private keys is essentially stored online in online wallets. Apart from easy accessibility, online wallets provide security against the failure of hardware and physical theft.

However, since all your information is stored online, it is prone to hackers and DDOS attacks. It is therefore essential to secure your cryptocurrency portfolio with a really strong password. With that said, many believe that you must not use an online wallet for large transactions because of the lack of security in these wallets.

To understand the concept of online wallets, let us take the example of storing your cryptocurrencies on a crypto exchange platform. If you store your digital currency on a crypto exchange, you should know that you won't be able to access your private key. In addition to this, if the crypto exchange platform gets hacked or shuts down, you will lose all your possessions stored on that platform.

This is why most cryptocurrency traders tend to have only as much money on crypto exchanges as they are going to actively trade. As a rule of thumb, any amount that you are not using on the exchange should be moved to a more secure cryptocurrency wallet.

Desktop Wallets

As their names suggest, desktop wallets are specially designed software that helps you store your public and private keys. A desktop wallet can be downloaded and installed on a computer, desktop, or laptop. In addition to this, a desktop wallet is only accessible on one system. This is what makes desktop wallets one of the most secure cryptocurrency wallets.

However, if you store your crypto assets on a desktop wallet, you should always be cautious of hackers and viruses. You must have a good antivirus in place to keep your desktop wallet safe and secure.

Desktop wallets for different types of cryptocurrencies are available for most operating systems. Although desktop wallets are not the most secure of wallets out there, they are relatively very easy to use. This installable program is more secure than online and mobile wallets. However, a user needs to create backup copies of their crypto assets on a separate hard disk. If you don't have a backup, you may not be able to recover any of your information in case your desktop fails or crashes.

Hardware Wallets

Known to be the most secure cryptocurrency wallets, hardware wallets are most commonly used by long-term investors. A hardware wallet can be understood as a device that is designed for cryptocurrency users to store their public addresses and private keys. A hardware wallet allows its users to store their crypto assets in a USB-like device. Hardware wallets are really easy to use. All you need to do is insert the device into your laptop or computer, log into your portfolio, and carry out the transactions.

Since all your crypto assets are stored on a secure device that is not connected to the internet, the hardware wallets provide the highest form of security for cryptocurrency users. However, a high level of security comes at a high price. Even the most basic of hardware wallets cost more than $150. With that said, a hardware wallet may have an external screen that shows your seed word along with storing your private keys securely.

In addition to this OLED screen, a hardware wallet may have buttons on the side that can be used to navigate through the options of the device. Apart from these features, most hardware wallets have a native desktop app that users can use to manage their assets and cryptocurrencies.

Mobile Wallets

Mobile wallets are one of the most commonly used wallets. Essentially, these wallets are applications that can be installed on mobile devices. Users can manage their crypto assets directly from their mobile phones, regardless of where they are, given that they have an internet connection. These wallets are specifically designed for retail transactions and to allow you to buy with digital currencies. In addition to this, mobile wallets are more compact and simpler than online or desktop wallets. However, since mobile phones can be lost or stolen, mobile wallets don't rank very high on safety. A mobile wallet user must save a backup of their crypto assets somewhere more secure. In addition to this, it is always a good habit to store only a certain amount of cryptocurrency on your phone that you are going to trade actively.

Block.io Wallet

This wallet is a versatile and secure place for your digital currency. Block.Io wallet supports multiple currencies and allows a user to conveniently manage several different cryptocurrencies in one place. In addition to this, the transaction via block.io wallet takes place instantly since everything happens through the blockchains. With that said, this platform also provides wallet hosting and customized support to all of its users. One of this wallet's best features is that a user is required to sign all of their transactions. Nobody else other than the user can carry out a transaction. In addition to this, this wallet provides fast and stable transactions with a quick response time and high uptime.

Exodus

Ideal for people just beginning to invest in cryptocurrency, this wallet is easy to use, secure, and interactive. Most mainstream cryptocurrency traders find this wallet to be great for cryptocurrency beginners. Exodus has a built-in exchange that can be accessed with just two taps on the screen and works on Android and iOS. This wallet allows users to monitor the cryptocurrency market movements on the go. In addition to this, you can sync your mobile application with the wallet's desktop version. With that said, This wallet allows users to access live charts and portfolios. However, the best thing about this wallet is that it provides 24/7 assistance to its users.

LoafWallet

Designed and promoted by the Litecoin Foundation company, LoafWallet is mainly used for trading Litecoin cryptocurrency (LTC). This wallet is lightweight in design and simple to use. In addition to this, this wallet's code is open source. With that said, this wallet employs a single payment verification method. With LoafWallet, Users can avoid the need for central service, accounts, and logins. This wallet generates all private keys and stores them locally on a device. And the best part is that the crypto assets can be covered if the device is stolen, broken, or lost.

How to Choose a Cryptocurrency Wallet

If you are just beginning in cryptocurrency trading, you will need to have a cryptocurrency wallet. While choosing a wallet, there are several factors to be considered. Although the best option for you depends on your preference, the process should involve practical and pragmatic aspects. There are several questions that you need to ask yourself before choosing a cryptocurrency wallet. You will have to think about what type of wallet you need, the underlying costs, the number of currencies you will hold, security, and convenience. This section will discover some factors that will assist you in choosing a good and secure cryptocurrency wallet.

Security

One of the prime deciding factors for your cryptocurrency wallet must be its security features. It is vital to prioritize security during a wallet selection. You must carry out plenty of research regarding the security offered by a potential cryptocurrency wallet before committing to it. With that said, if you want to opt for the most secure cryptocurrency wallet, hardware wallets can help you ensure the best measures for safety.

Fees

Although most cryptocurrency wallets are free to use, some wallets may require you to invest. This is usually the case with hardware wallets. The cost will increase as per your needs and requirements. While it may cost you some money to get a hardware wallet to manage your crypto assets, they provide the highest level of security. In addition to this, this type of wallet is best for long-term investors. The additional cost comes with an increase in security. If cost is no matter to you, you must invest in hardware wallets just to be on the safer side of things.

Multi-Currency Support

One of the most important features that you should look for in a cryptocurrency wallet is multi-currency support. This will help you hold more than one type of cryptocurrency. It is convenient to have all your crypto assets in one place. In addition to this, it is best to research a wallet's features and read reviews online before finalizing it. If a wallet supports multiple cryptocurrencies, you can easily manage all of your digital currencies and portfolios. However, if you're planning to hold just one cryptocurrency, it is best to visit the website and look for a dedicated wallet.

Backup Feature

If you are using a mobile or online wallet, you risk losing your investments if your phone is stolen or broken. To avoid incurring huge losses, it is vital to ensure that the cryptocurrency wallet offers distinct backup services. In most top cryptocurrency wallets, You will find adequate backup procedures, including several passphrases, rescue links, and passwords to recover your crypto assets. In addition to the backup features, a good cryptocurrency wallet will have a two-factor authentication security feature to block an unauthorized user from accessing your account.

Additional Features

If a cryptocurrency wallet is open source and allows people to review their entire code, it can mean a good thing. If there are any problems in the wallet structure, they will be easily identified and reported. In addition to this, the bugs in a new cryptocurrency wallet can be eliminated if it is open-source. With that said, While choosing a cryptocurrency wallet, you must consider its mobility as well. If you want to have access to your crypto assets from anywhere at any given time, you will benefit from having a mobile or online wallet.

To conclude this chapter, let's take a glance at the key takeaways from this chapter. A cryptocurrency wallet can be a hardware, software, or digital service to help you store your crypto assets like transaction history, public addresses, and private keys. There are plenty of wallets to choose from. The different types of wallets include paper, desktop, online, mobile, hardware, block.io, LoafWallet, and Exodus wallet.

With that done, we discovered the most important factors to be considered while choosing a cryptocurrency wallet. Security, fees, mobility, convenience, backup features, and multi-currency support are some important barometers that you should utilize while choosing a cryptocurrency wallet for yourself. Although the best wallet for you depends upon your needs and requirements, you can use the various measuring factors mentioned in this chapter to help you decide on a convenient one.

Chapter 6: Cryptocurrency Trading Platforms

Cryptocurrency trading platforms should have three important factors: strong security, a user-friendly platform, and access to a variety of cryptocurrencies.

Coinbase

Coinbase is one of the more established cryptocurrency trading platforms. It is US-based and trades in more than 50 cryptocurrencies. The platform is available in all US states except Hawaii. When using Coinbase, you can trade either on their original platform or on Coinbase Pro. Coinbase Pro offers 59 cryptocurrencies compared to the 56 on the original platform. It also offers advanced charting functions and allows you to carry out crypto-to-crypto transactions.

Its fee system is a little confusing and depends on two things. Firstly, Coinbase charges around 0.5% for crypto trades, and this can fluctuate depending on the market. Secondly, the platform charges a flat fee or a variable fee (whichever is greater).

Here is a little guide as to how their fees work from Coinbase themselves. If the trade amount is $10 or less, the fee would be $0.99. For a trade over $10 up to $25. The fee would be $1.49. The other fees include the payment type - the only fee method would be an ACH transfer. To make a payment into a U.S. bank account or Coinbase wallet, the fee is around 1.49%, and to pay it into a debit card, the fee is 3.99%.

The Coinbase Pro fee structure is more straightforward. The fees you're charged depend on your monthly trading volume and liquidity of the asset when you bought it. Both deposits and withdrawals must be made through a bank account - card purchases are not allowed on Coinbase Pro.

Coinbase provides over 60 crypto-to-crypto trading pairs. There are over 40 currencies that can trade for bitcoin, 7 that can trade with Ethereum, and 11 that can trade with USDC. USDC is Coinbase's own crypto and is a stable cryptocurrency that is linked to the US dollar.

Security is a major factor when choosing a trading platform. Although the SIPC or the FDIC does not protect cryptocurrency traders, Coinbase assures that their digital currency is insured. They have advised that they keep less than 2% of funds online and that and the rest of its customers' funds are stored offline, in cold storage. This helps keep it safe from any online hacks. The insurance is in place so that if anything were to happen, they would be able to cover any financial losses. This insurance, however, does not cover breaches related to individual accounts, like the compromising of your password.

Coinbase has never proved that they have a reserve fund and have refused to take part in any audits concerning this.

The app is available on both iOS and Android and has a high rating. The app has many of the same functions as the desktop site.

To conclude the pros and cons, the pros are that you can trade with over 50 cryptos, there is a low minimum to start, and your funds are insured in case Coinbase is hacked. The con is that they have higher fees when compared with other crypto platforms.

Kraken

Kraken provides crypto trading, futures contracts, and margin trading. This platform is based in the US and therefore must comply with the state's regulation, so they only offer around 20 cryptocurrencies. As Kraken offers more advanced attributes like margin trading, this platform is great for experienced traders. The fees are fairly average, and these drop rapidly once you start trading over $50,000 a month in volume.

Everyone in the US, except residents of New York or Washington State, can use Kraken. International traders based in Afghanistan, Cuba, Iran, Iraq, Japan, Tajikistan, and North Korea cannot use this platform.

Kraken's fees are pretty fair - if you are trading less than $50,000 a month in volume, you will pay around a 0.16% maker fee and a 0.26% taker fee. The more volume per month, the more discounted this rate gets.

This platform supports crypto deposits and allows for unlimited deposits even if you haven't undergone a

KYC verification. The only limits are on withdrawals. A deposit can only be funded through a bank or wire transfer. Currently, deposits cannot earn interest.

The security of this trading platform is pretty strong, and they have claimed that 95% of their deposits are kept offline in cold storage. They also advise that they keep complete reserves, so you can make withdrawals whenever you like. These reserves have been audited, so it can be proven that they exist. Kraken is the only crypto trading platform to prove that they have reserves.

They support 2-factor authentication and withdrawals, and confirmations are available via email. They have a great track record regarding the security of the platform and have their own security team. Kraken has been hacked and appears to take security seriously, so they are one of the safer platforms around.

Kraken does not have the greatest track record for customer service as it seems that they have slow response times over chat and email.

Their margin trading is one of their best features, as is their low trading fees. This platform is one of the more affordable crypto exchanges based in America.

Binance

This platform is based in Malta and is often viewed as one of the biggest platforms for trading volumes. On this platform, you have access to over 540 crypto-to-crypto trades. It was previously only exclusively dealing in crypto-crypto trades. However, they now offer fiat deposits or withdrawals. Fiat deposits and withdrawals are only available via credit cards or bank transfers. Not every location is eligible to use this, so you should check this prior.

Binance has relatively low trading fees, standard fees are around 0.1%, but this number is reduced when holding the Binance Coin. The lowest trading fee available is 0.04%, but this means you would have to trade 150,000 Binance Coins in one month.

The platform used to accept almost everyone. However, it is currently closed off to those holding a US passport. This is because it is looking to launch an exchange solely for US citizens that complies with regulations. If you are from the United States, you will have to wait until they have launched this to begin using this platform.

Binance offers 2-factor authentication to keep your account secure. If you attempt to log in from a device that you have not previously used, you will have to confirm this via email. You will also receive emails when important functions are carried out.

A form of insurance Binance offers is the SAFU (Secure Asset Fund for Users). This came around in 2018 and is a reserve fund that will be used in the case that Binance is hacked. 10% of all trading fees are used to fund SAFU. In 2019, Binance was, in fact, hacked. However, the fund was able to cover any users who would have otherwise faced a loss.

Binance is known for having great customer service, which comes in handy if you're a beginner or you need to confirm or check something as soon as possible.

It's not hard to see how Binance has become one of the largest crypto trading platforms, from the hundreds of crypto-to-crypto pairs to the low trading fees and amplified security. It can now host Fiat deposits and withdrawals, although this is currently only available to users in a select number of locations.

Gemini

Gemini is a US-based platform complete with FDIC protection for USD. This platform is fairly easy to use and places security at the top of its priorities. Notably, it appears to have never been hacked. This platform is available in all 50 states of the US and over 50 countries worldwide.

They offer over 30 cryptocurrencies, including their own currency, Gemini dollars. Gemini has partnered with Samsung, which means that users based in the US and Canada are able to connect their Samsung Blockchain Wallet to their Gemini app to trade.

You have to fund your Gemini account through your bank account, not with a debit or credit card. You can earn interest on your crypto. Currently, this goes up to

7% on different currencies. For Bitcoin, the interest rate is around 3.05%.

The app is fairly easy to use when compared to the desktop site. However, if you want to make more complex trades, it is probably better to use the site. The app is free, available on both iOS and Android, and has a high rating in the AppStore.

Trading minimums depend on the type of currency you are trading - for Bitcoin trades, the minimum is 0.00001 Bitcoin, and for Ethereum, it is 0.001.

Gemini charges a convenience fee that is 0.50% above the market rate. To figure out potential fees, you will need to multiply 0.50% by the amount of currency you want to buy. They also have a flat transaction fee when you place orders which starts at $0.99 to 1.49% of your order value. Gemini does not, however, charge transaction fees for deposits.

If you do not currently have a crypto wallet, Gemini offers its own Gemini Wallet. This will be protected against losses that arise from a security breach or hack. Having insurance for your digital assets is a great benefit, especially if you are new to crypto trading. However, any losses that occur due to your own security breaches are not covered by their insurance.

Gemini has never proved its reserves though some believe they have built it through fractional reserve banking of customer funds.

Gemini's selling point is the fact they place safety so highly. It is also US-based and has an easy-to-use platform. It does, however, have higher fees than some other platforms.

Although it has slightly higher fees than other trading platforms, its security features, and easy-to-use interface balance this out. It is marketed as "simple, elegant, and secure," which makes it great if you are new to the crypto world and want to dip your toes in.

CashApp

CashApp began as a way for payments to be sent between people. It has now grown into a comprehensive banking system. Debit cards cannot be attached to the app, ACH transfers received, as well as investing in the traditional stock market.

This app also offers an option to trade Bitcoin in their buying and selling stocks section. Users were able to trade bitcoin even before they could trade traditional stocks.

Bitcoin can be easily bought and sold on the app. However, the trading fees are pretty much unknown at the point of trade. These fees depend on the market and can fluctuate. There are two different fees, and one is around the current vitality of the bitcoin price. Usually, the fees for selling and buying bitcoin via this app are around 1.75% or 2%.

What's so rare about this app is the bitcoin integration - users can buy bitcoin within seconds and withdraw it into a non-custodial wallet. It has never been easy to buy and sell bitcoin.

The bitcoin left on the app can, however, be subject to being seized or suspended. CashApp has full control of your bitcoin on the app, so it is best to transfer it to your wallet once you have bought it.

The app is only available in the US and the UK, so only the US dollar and the British pound are supported. According to CashApp, bitcoin will continue to play a huge role in its expansion.

The pros of this app are that it is very easy to buy and hold bitcoin, it is also fast and simple to use. However, it is still fairly limited in features, and some markets are unable to get their hands on a CashApp card or buy bitcoin.

Uphold

Uphold is well-known for its ability to offer "anything-to-anything" trades. This means you can trade assets directly using a bank account, debit card, etc. All with no trading commissions. You can also trade between assets. For example, you can trade Bitcoin to Tesla without there needing to be any transfers in between.

This one-stop ordering means your account must be funded through a transfer from your bank account or purchasing with a credit card. This will then be converted into the equivalent value of the current or asset you want to buy. Uphold allows you to buy cryptocurrencies and even precious metals without needing funds to clear.

You can send money or other assets to friends or family without any additional fees. You can send cryptocurrencies within seconds, and these transfers are always free. Uphold is incredibly cost-effective, with 0% deposit fees, trading commission, and withdrawal fees. This doesn't mean it is completely free to use - they add a small spread to the price that you can see at preview. The exchange fee you are charged depends on the asset that is being converted.

Uphold also offers the Uphold card, on which you can spend precious metals, bitcoin, or any other asset you have in the form of cash. The Uphold card is a MasterCard debit card and is accepted in most places worldwide.

Their app is simple and mirrors the desktop site, allowing you to carry out their "anything-to-anything" transfers. The app holds live data from the market, and the price is usually calculated to the 5th decimal, helping you make informed choices. It is pretty easy to open up an account and use the platform. Around 36 cryptocurrencies are available on this app.

Their low fees and straightforward transactions are attractive to people who send money internationally on a regular basis. Their platform is easy to use, and their unique "anything-to-anything" trades make them incredibly unique. They do, however, lack educational resources on their platform, and it may be hard to contact customer service in a timely manner as they do not have a phone line.

TradeStation

As an advanced trader, this platform is great. It currently offers $0 trades in an attempt to draw in casual traders. As a serious investor, this is a solid choice. At one point, they only catered for professional brokers and money managers. Now, your ordinary investor has access to these tools.

This platform offers commission-free trades, although users must have a $2,000 minimum balance. For high-volume traders, the pricing structure is either per-share/per-contract commissions or unbundled pricing.

The platform's tools are some of the most comprehensive in the market. It has an incredibly impressive platform and provides direct market access and tools for users to be able to design, test, monitor, and automate their trading strategies. You can even customize your desktop with a wide array of colors. However, their layout makes it fairly difficult to easily navigate the platform. This can be fairly frustrating, especially if you are looking for an easy-to-use interface.

Their app mirrors their desktop site, and you can make trades, place orders, and carry out research. If you travel often, this could be great. They also provide live data streaming, notification features, and it's fairly easy to create a watchlist. One of the greatest features of this platform is how exhaustive its educational tools are. They offer different forms of educational resources such as e-books or video demonstrations.

You can test out new trading strategies without actually having to use real money, using their simulator tool. The cryptocurrencies that can be traded are bitcoin, bitcoin cash, Ethereum, Litecoin, and Ripple.

As an active and experienced trader, this platform can work really well. However, their plans and pricing can be a little confusing. It's not the best platform for those starting out in the crypto world, as their initial focus is on professional brokers.

Take stock of the cryptocurrency trading platforms above, and work out what is important to you. Trading crypto has become so much more popular, which means that crypto exchanges will get better, more secure, and user-friendly. This gives you the confidence you need to trade and puts your mind at ease.

Chapter 7: Technical Analysis

Whether you are looking to invest in a cryptocurrency to earn a profit in the long run through a gradual increase in share price or to start trading a volatile cryptocurrency to earn profits in the short run, without a solid analysis to base your investment decisions on, making a profit will not be possible. In other forms of trading, such as stock trading, both fundamental analysis, and technical analysis are used.

However, when it comes to cryptocurrencies, it is the technical analysis that is more beneficial. Moreover, fundamental analysis is aimed at understanding the nature of a company and how profitable its operations are. This valuation of its performance influences the share price, and in the case of cryptocurrencies, there is no business to evaluate, so technical analysis is the way to go.

Basics of Technical Analysis

As the name implies, the technical analysis aims to evaluate a cryptocurrency on a technical level and understand how a certain one will be priced in the future. To evaluate a cryptocurrency, technical analysts employ a wide variety of mathematical formulas and statistical representations to understand the price behavior of a certain one and forecast its future.

To fully understand the technical approach, you must keep in mind three of the main assumptions that technical analysis assumes necessary to understand the overall methodology.

Assumptions

1. Prices move in defined and predictable trends

2. The market accurately depicts the sentiment of investors

3. Trends from the past will be repeated in the future

Keeping these things in mind, we will look at different charts used in technical analysis, which look at previous prices, previous trading volumes of a certain cryptocurrency, and then see what we can predict.

There are many different types of charts that can be used, each one telling a story about a different aspect of cryptocurrency. Moreover, some types of graphs and charts, such as candlestick charts, bar charts, and line charts, can be used to understand the same data. In effect, they are statistically illustrating the same information, but the difference in how this information is shown can impact our analysis. There is no hard and fast rule about what should or should not be used - the kind of analysis tools that one uses is subjective.

Types of Charts

Charts can show information about one or more cryptocurrencies on one graph, though not all charts can be used to illustrate multiple cryptocurrencies simultaneously. In essence, all charts aim to show how the amount of trade that took place for a certain cryptocurrency varied at different price points over a certain time period. On the horizontal axis is the time and the vertical axis marks the price. These charts can be used to look at very short movements spanning a few minutes or very long movements spanning several months or even years.

Here are some of the most commonly used charts.

1. Line Charts

The line chart is a very basic and easy-to-understand chart that analysts widely use to get a basic understanding of a cryptocurrency's price behavior. The line chart is used to track the closing price of a commodity over a certain period of time. If you are looking at a 24-hour chart, the chart will show the closing price at every hour during the 24-hour period. If you connect all the plotted dots, you get a line that shows the overall price trend for that day. This is a great chart to use if you are only looking for the price trend, but since it only takes into account the closing price, it doesn't offer much insight into the intraday price movements.

2. Bar Charts

The bar chart is similar to the line chart, but the way that each price point is illustrated offers a lot more insight than the line chart. At each point, which was previously just a dot, a vertical line has two more lines extending out on either side of it.

The highest point of the vertical line shows the highest price at which the commodity traded at that point in time during the day, whereas the lowermost point of the vertical line shows the lowest price at which the cryptocurrency traded that day. The horizontal line extending left from the vertical line shows the price at which trading started during the day, and the horizontal extending right shows the price at which trading closed. Moreover, the length of the vertical line shows the range of the price movement that the cryptocurrency went through.

In this way, the bar chart offers a lot more information about the cryptocurrency and gives a more in-depth picture of how the currency is traded during the day.

3. Candlestick Charts

When you see the way these charts represent the information, they look just like a candlestick, which has a thick trunk section and thinner lines extending both above and below the center part. These are very popular with technical analysts as they represent a lot of information in a very concise manner. They offer all the information that bar charts show, such as highs, lows, opening, and closing prices, but the main difference is that while bar charts only show the information for a single day, these can show information for a much wider time range. Moreover, the color of the candlestick also changes based on the price movement.

A falling candlestick is generally represented with a black or red body, while a rising candlestick is either clear or white. In the context of a rising candlestick, the thin line extending above the candlestick's body shows the highest price that was achieved, while the point at which it connects to the candlestick body shows the closing price for the day.

The line extending below the candlestick shows the lowest price that was achieved, and the point at which it meets the candlestick's body is where trading opened. The real body, or the candlestick itself, shows the range of prices through which the cryptocurrency fluctuated during that day. In the case of a falling candlestick, all these points are inverted.

Significance of Psychology of the Trader

The mindset and the psychology of the trader have a big impact on how well they can execute trades and eventually how much money they can make. When we say that you need to maintain a balanced mindset while you trade, this is reflected in how well you can stick to your trading plan, how cautious you are of the risks involved, how aware you are of unexpected market changes, and how emotionally detached you are from the trading. A person with a calm mind will be more responsible as they trade and will be very realistic and objective when making decisions. Poor trading psychology is one of the main reasons traders fail to profit and often dig themselves deeper into a hole of loss. While good traders rarely get anxious, those with poor psychology constantly worry about every decision they take and are a nervous wreck when trading.

Moreover, weak traders often do what is known as revenge trading, where they are trying to fight other traders, or even the market, by their trading, which only hurts them and no one else. They don't spend any time evaluating their own performance, introspecting, and then developing their weaknesses. They are so focused on trying to profit that they get caught up in emotion and make little progress as traders. They are easily distracted by fear and greed and are more likely to self-sabotage.

Main Types of Trends

When analysts and traders look at the various charts, they are looking for a trend in the market as their investment decisions will be based on these trends, depending on the approach that they take. Generally, there are either upward trends or downward trends. The former shows that a commodity's price is rising while the latter shows that the overall price is falling. With an upward trend, the price may spike up and down, but the price movement will be upwards when you look at the 100-day average or any longer-term average. The opposite is true for a downward trend.

This is important because, through technical analysis, we are trying to identify swings and pivots. Swing points are either high or low points between which the price of a commodity is 'swinging.' Pivot points are those points from which the price either pivots upwards into a swing at a higher price bracket or pivots down to a swing in a lower price range. These different points mark various points where different investors may choose to enter or exit the trade.

The Key Levels

Other than swing and pivot points, traders are also very interested in understanding the support and resistance points. As a technical analyst, these are arguably the most important things to look out for. Essentially, the support and resistance points are prices at which the cryptocurrency faces a barrier that restricts the price from moving in a certain direction.

Support points are what prices in a downtrend are looking for, and they find these points of support when the price reaches a point where it finds demand. On the other hand, a resistance point is a level that a price in an upward trend would encounter when it reaches a stage where it meets competitive supply. Once these areas of support and resistance have been identified, they serve as entry and exit points for investors. People will generally assume that the price will not surpass the support or resistance points, though it often does. In the case that it does surpass these points, the investor will either sell out to minimize loss or hold on to the currency to enjoy profits.

If you look at the price behavior of a cryptocurrency, in the long run, you will notice that these support and resistance points do frequently change, though if you can accurately identify them, it makes trading that much more profitable.

Indicators

To get a more in-depth view of the price behavior of a certain cryptocurrency, traders rely on various technical indicators, which tell us more about how the price of a commodity is changing over time, and these indicators also tell us about the demand and supply of the commodity. While trends and price levels have their own significance, these are some of the most common indicators that are very helpful in trading.

Moving Averages

Moving averages even out the extreme highs and lows at the price of a commodity and give the reader the average price change through a certain time period. Like the other charts used, moving average prices of a commodity can be seen for different time frames. Some might choose to see the variation in price averages for just a few minutes or hours, while others may choose to get a more holistic idea by looking at average price changes through the course of a few months or even a year. Most commonly, traders choose to look at the 50-day, 100-day, and 200-day moving price average. Using these three averages gives us a well-rounded image of how a cryptocurrency is performing and how it is likely to behave in the future.

Basic Moving Averages

Moving averages can be further divided into basic moving averages, known as simple moving averages, and sophisticated moving averages, known as exponential moving averages.

Basic moving averages take into account the price overall for a long duration. They are calculated by adding the lowest and the highest prices that a cryptocurrency was traded at and dividing it by the total number of averages. A five-day simple moving average will add the highest and lowest prices of the past five days and divide it by the number of days, giving you the basic moving average.

Sophisticated Moving Averages

These are also known as exponential moving averages since they are measured with a higher weightage allotted to recent price changes. For this reason, exponential price averages are more relevant to people who are looking at recent price changes. Even if you are studying price changes over a long duration, the findings will be more heavily influenced by recent price changes with exponential moving averages. The way this is calculated is more complex than basic moving averages, but if you have the right information, you can still calculate this on your own. When you compare the simple moving average and the exponential moving average for the same period for a cryptocurrency that is in an upward trend, the exponential price average will appear to be higher.

Bollinger Bands

The Bollinger Bands are a type of chart indicator that is used in conjunction with moving price averages. They are also considered to be price envelopes of the moving price average as the bands 'envelope' the moving price average line on a graph. This cloud or envelope that extends above and below each point on the moving average line shows the upper and lower extreme of where the price could go. However, there are more in-depth uses of the Bollinger bands depending on how they are applied.

The Bollinger band consists of three lines, which are calculated individually. The value commonly used for the centerline, which is the basis for the two outlying lines, is the 20-day simple moving average. In some cases, a more complex calculation goes into determining the centerline, but as a basic measurement, the 20-day moving average will work just fine. The upper line is calculated by adding twice the daily standard deviation to the middle line. Similarly, the lower line is calculated by subtracting twice the daily standard deviation from the middle line. As a result, we now have the centerline with a corresponding upper and lower outlying line.

One of the main things that Bollinger bands are used to analyze is overbought and oversold conditions. An oversold condition occurs when the prices of a commodity break through the lower Bollinger band, in which case they are likely to bounce back up again. On the other hand, an overbought condition arises when the market price exceeds the upper Bollinger band, which is when the price can be expected to retract back to lower levels.

However, these two types of Bollinger band analyses are used on the premise that the market price of a cryptocurrency will follow the concept of mean reversion. Mean reversion implies that when a price sways significantly higher or lower than the mean or average price, sooner or later, it will revert to the average price. In situations where the market price is swinging within a certain price bracket, or the entire market is range-bound, this can be a useful insight.

Even though the Bollinger band is a useful statistic to use, it should be kept in mind that it does have its limitations, and its results are best used in specific market conditions. For currencies that don't follow these market trends, these bands can be counterproductive.

Chapter 8: Why Invest and What Are the Risks?

Cryptocurrency has witnessed remarkable growth in the last few years. However, some people still view cryptocurrency with caution and have a limited understanding of what it is. However, investing in cryptocurrency can be a good idea. Cryptocurrency is risky, but it has the potential for high returns. This chapter discusses the reasons why you should consider investing in cryptocurrency. It also highlights the risks involved in cryptocurrency.

High Returns

Cryptocurrency has been around for a short time, but it has been touted as highly profitable compared to other forms of investment. A cryptocurrency can immediately show solid changes in prices over very short periods. For instance, you can expect to get a return of about 20% of your investment which is a fair result. It is not easy to find these high-profit levels when you decide to trade in other assets.

However, to succeed in crypto trading, you must have a solid strategy to use as a framework. Just like any other kind of trade that you may think of, crypto trading requires you to have a plan. In this plan, you should outline your goals and what you aim to achieve within a certain period. The chances of losing money will be very high if you try to trade in cryptocurrency without a meaningful strategy.

Transformational Technology

Cryptocurrency is also known as digital technology, and it can be a game-changer in the global economy. The blockchain technology that underlies different cryptocurrencies can impact various industries like healthcare, shipping, banking, and supply chains. Cryptocurrency does not rely on intermediaries like fiat currency when performing transactions across borders. The distributed ledgers that strongly depend on computer networks make cryptocurrency independent.

With cryptocurrency, you can buy directly from another business in a different country, and you can perform the transaction directly. If you perform a wire transfer involving fiat money, it could end up going through various banks, and the entire process can be expensive. The exchange rate involving different currencies can also affect the ultimate price you pay for doing business with other global companies.

Cryptocurrencies promise a smooth passage of transactions within borders without the involvement of regulatory authorities like banks. Cryptocurrencies can make attractive investment opportunities for people interested in earning high returns while at the same time supporting new technology. Regardless of geographical boundary, you can use cryptocurrency of your choice from any place without the hassles of foreign currency exchange rates that are often distorted.

Cryptocurrency is a global currency that can revolutionize the financial services sector and banking without paying high fees. Enlightened businesses are accepting cryptocurrencies as a form of payment in different places around the world. As time goes on, there are chances that the "digital gold" will make sweeping changes to the global economies. Therefore, investing now in digital currency can give you a comfortable seat as we move into the future that is characterized by constant changes.

Store of Value

Gold is commonly viewed as a stable store of value among different types of precious minerals. Bitcoin, in particular, is regarded as the "digital gold" due to its censorship-resistant and deflationary properties. If you are worried about issues like bank failures, natural disaster scenarios, and hyperinflationary events, you can invest in cryptocurrency.

You have observed in Chapter 3 that cryptocurrency is created through the process known as crypto mining. This process involves the use of computers to solve sophisticated puzzles, and a group of miners usually does it. Unlike fiat currency, this simply means that cryptocurrency comes in limited supply since mathematical algorithms are used to cap it. In other words, it means that it is not easy to create cryptocurrency like paper money that can be printed without anything to back it.

Politicians and central governments often resort to printing fiat currency to satisfy their egos, but this often leads to inflation. Oversupply of money in the market erodes its value. However, no single government can wield control or dilute the value of cryptocurrency, which can subsequently lead to inflation.

Cryptocurrency Is Based on Speculation

The price of cryptocurrency is usually determined by speculation, and this can help you generate high profits from your trade. Many investors buy cryptocurrencies in anticipation that the value will increase. Therefore, if you buy and hold your cryptocurrency, you are likely to generate more profit when you sell it shortly.

Elements like speculation strongly determine all types of trade. Since crypto trading is still a new concept, speculative behavior should be expected. However, traders need to be careful and avoid falling into traps like herd instinct and Greater Fool Fallacy. There is a difference between a foolish risk and a calculated one.

No-One Can Take Your Cryptocurrency

Naturally, cryptocurrency is cryptographic, which means that no government can confiscate your crypto without your cooperation. Cryptocurrency offers you a high level of independence that you can never do with fiat money. When you bank your money, you can wake up with nothing or valueless notes when the money is eroded by inflation. The other problem with fiat currency is that the bank can go bankrupt or be robbed, affecting all depositors.

However, with cryptocurrency, you are 100% secure since no one can tamper with your crypto. No financial institution is required to keep your cryptocurrency or to facilitate any transaction where you can end up being charged exorbitant fees. It can be observed that cryptocurrency can decentralize the global economy where a few powerful countries do not control it. You can invest in cryptocurrency now if you want to enjoy hassle-free transactions.

High Liquidity

Cryptocurrency consists of high liquidity, which means that it is easy to buy or sell. There are different tools that you can use when trading cryptocurrencies which make it easy to trade them. Tools such as limit order or automated buying and selling help protect your investment. You can use the option to cap the limit of currency that you want to trade. The good thing about this strategy is that it automatically stops when you reach the expected ceiling of your trade.

The other important aspect is that it is easy to join in trading cryptocurrency. You do not necessarily need to deal with any institution like a bank or sign any papers. All you need to do is create an account on the preferred platform, depending on the type of crypto you want to trade in. After creating a wallet, the next thing is to learn how to trade using a demo account. When you are ready, you can begin trading and track your assets, and this stage is very simple.

Favorable Forecasts

Every trade comes with some risks that can lead to loss of money. Price fluctuations and market volatility are very common, and they significantly impact your trade. Short-term losses in crypto trading can be hard-hitting, but it is easier to study the trend in crypto trading. Many forecasts in crypto trading indicate that investing in the long term can reap significant benefits in the next three to five years.

Many cryptocurrencies are undergoing a downward trend, but there are indications that the prices will once again shoot up. Therefore, you can capitalize on this potentially high-return investment though it comes with high risks. The benefits that you will get are likely to offset the risks that you are likely to face when you make a long-term investment.

Investing in cryptocurrency can go a long way in helping you diversify your portfolio. This will help you gain a better understanding of how the world of cryptocurrency functions. Once you involve yourself in crypto trading, you will gain significant hands-on experience, which will help you make informed decisions. Once you take part in crypto trading, you are also likely to research different topics that will help broaden your understanding of digital currencies. You need to choose your investment wisely and know that cryptocurrencies are not created equal. Do your research first and make sure that you choose the right crypto that can give you leverage to succeed in your trade.

Common Features of Cryptocurrencies

As you have observed in this section, cryptocurrencies generally share some similarities that you should know. As a recap, the following things that you should know before you decide to invest in cryptocurrency.

- Cryptocurrency constitutes transformative technology that can transform the industry
- Crypto provides a safe store of value
- Offers high profitability
- High liquidity
- Your cryptocurrency cannot be tampered with.

You need to show some keen interest to learn if you want to succeed in crypto trading.

Investing Mindset

If you want to become a successful investor, then you should start by developing the right mindset. You should build a strong investing mindset and be prepared for tough situations that you are likely to encounter. If you want to succeed in your endeavor, you must have a sound financial plan and the right frame of mind. If you are a newbie in crypto trading, you should treat it as a business like any other type of trade.

Essentially, you aim to generate some profits from your trade, and this is the major driving factor that should help you draw your investment plans. With the right plan, you can avoid costly mistakes that can impact your success. Controlling the market is beyond our capability, but we can control our investment. This means that you must have a viable strategy that you must follow if you want to reach your desired goals.

In short, your investing mindset tips include the following factors:

- Create a financial plan
- Do not deviate from your financial plan
- Do not be guided by emotions
- Aim for the big picture
- Buy and ignore
- Avoid chasing the next big thing

When you are investing in cryptocurrency, it is vital to ensure that you do not change your plan in response to sudden market changes. You must focus on your long-term goals, and you will realize that you can easily achieve your goals. Markets are volatile, so you must concentrate on your goals and objectives to increase your chances of success. Shifting goalposts is a recipe for disaster that you should not entertain.

Initial Coin Offering

In the cryptocurrency industry, an initial coin offering is more like an initial public offering (IPO). ICO is when a company looks for ways to raise funds after launching a service, app, or new coin. The investors can buy the offering, and they will receive a token in the form of cryptocurrency offered by the company. The token can come with some utility value, or it can just be a representation of a stake within the company's project.

Startups that want to offer new services or products related to blockchain technology or cryptocurrency make use of ICOs. The ICOs can offer great potential to the investors to earn massive yields, but they can turn out to be fraud if not managed properly. It is vital to buy digital currency first if you want to participate in ICO. Other ICOs can turn out to be fraud, so you must exercise caution before you venture into this area. This sector is unregulated.

Losses, Scams, and Theft

Trading in cryptocurrency sounds impressive, but it is not free from other risks like theft and scams. The risk that you are likely to face concerning cryptocurrency is that a central intermediary does not control it. This means that the onus is on you to take safety measures to store your cryptographic keys that help control the blockchain address. If fiat currency is damaged, it is replaced by the central bank. However, failure to adhere to security measures to protect your cryptocurrency can compromise its safety.

Other threats that you are likely to face pertain to issues like hacking. Hacking is widespread, and hackers constantly refine their tactics to steal money and confidential information from unsuspecting online users. To date, hackers have stolen several tokens of cryptocurrency from ordinary users, wallet software, and other exchanges. Scammers also use different schemes to hoodwink the users to provide their tokens.

Fake ICOs are also commonly used by scammers to steal from unsuspecting crypto investors. Cybercriminals and hackers are turning their focus to digital currencies, and issues like phishing, money laundering, and cyber-attacks are becoming widespread in the world of cryptocurrency. Security breaches are also a common occurrence as hackers try to steal confidential data from unsuspecting traders.

The other challenge with cryptocurrency is that the users can forget passwords, and this can lead to irreversible loss. You cannot reset your digital wallet as you do with other applications. Therefore, when you lose your password, you are bound to lose your digital currency. Many people have lost millions worth of cryptocurrency as a result of issues related to lost devices or forgotten passwords.

Cryptocurrency Is Extremely Volatile

Crypto trading is highly volatile, and this is one of the biggest risks that you should be wary of. For instance, Bitcoin, at some point, lost more than 80% of this value in one go. The value of Bitcoin fell from around $20,000 to a measly $3,000. The cryptocurrency market can be extremely volatile, and investing in this sector can be stressful if you are risk-aversive. Crypto trading can succeed over time, but few investors can stomach the short-term changes they are likely to experience in their trading journey.

There is still a long way for cryptocurrency to gain trust and acceptance by the generality of consumers and merchants. As it stands, digital currency needs some form of stability to help in determining a fair price of different goods. For example, the dramatic fall of bitcoin's value in the above example leaves a conundrum. People are less likely to spend bitcoins like the way they do with other fiat currencies as a result of their volatility.

Crypto Trading Is Based on Speculation

To a larger extent, speculation is the major factor that drives people into undertaking different types of trade. Whatever asset you decide to trade, your bets are based on speculation where you anticipate that trade can go your way, and you achieve a favorable result. While speculation is good for investment, you cannot get any guarantee that the trend will continue to perform in the same way in the long term.

The main problem with cryptocurrency is that it is a relatively new form of investment, making it riskier than other types of stocks. It is still to be proved if cryptocurrencies will gain popularity like fiat currencies or the hype will fade away in a few years. This uncertainty can make trading in cryptocurrency riskier than other forms of investment.

Other Risks

Other risks are associated with owning crypto. You cannot trade cryptocurrency on the traditional stock market exchange, making it difficult to deal with. Most cryptocurrencies are traded via crypto exchanges, and some of them do not exchange with cash. You may also need a special digital wallet to keep your coins so that you can exchange them for cash. Cryptocurrency cannot be a trusted method of holding value since it is something intangible. Up to date, it is still not very clear what backs the value of cryptocurrency. The value of fiat currency is determined by gold reserves stored somewhere in the vaults at the central bank.

In this chapter, you familiarized yourself with all the reasons why some people remain skeptical about digital currencies regardless of their promise to offer high returns. Many people view the blockchain as a transformative industry that is capable of disrupting the global economy like the advent of the internet did in the 1990s. However, you need to be careful and understand the risks involved before you invest in cryptocurrency. You need to understand the complex security issues involved in digital currency. You must take your time to learn the common pitfalls that many crypto investors usually make.

Chapter 9: Trading Strategies for Beginners

"Paper money is going away" - Elon Musk

Have you been following the crypto market lately? Are you intrigued by the lucrative aspect of trading? Do you want to enter the cryptocurrency market but don't have a strategy yet? The strategies you choose to utilize for trading can make or break your business. There's no doubt that digital currency is the future of money.

People from all over the world understand this. This is a reason why cryptocurrency traders are breaking records. Almost everyone who watches the news knows how profitable trading in cryptocurrency can be. Although there are a lot of big-shot investors who doubt the success of cryptocurrency, the constant rise in crypto rates cannot be ignored.

The cryptocurrency market may encounter frequent dips and highs, but that's what makes it so attractive. If you follow the right strategies and take the time to understand the nitty-gritty of cryptocurrency trading, you can earn a fortune in a surprisingly short time. If you are a beginner in cryptocurrency trading, this chapter will help you understand the most common and basic strategies used by experienced traders.

In this chapter, you'll discover some superb short-term trading strategies. In addition to this, you'll learn about the concept of time frames and a few methods used for analyzing short-term trading. With that said, this informative chapter will guide you through the strategies used for long-term trading and methods to expand and diversify your portfolio. By the end of this chapter, you'll be able to trade safely, profitably and learn to manage the risks involved in trading.

Strategies for Short-Term Trading

The main objective of short-term trading is to earn a decent profit by buying and selling large quantities of low-priced stocks. It all comes down to being on a constant lookout for potential candidates that can earn you a good profit. In addition to this, you need to be aware of the stocks that you must avoid.

With that said, a lot of investors fall into the trap of believing the information they find on the streets or the news. Regardless of how solid a tip is, you must always research yourself. The following trading tips found in the financial pages of a magazine are not always profitable because, by the time you get the information, the market is already reacting to it. This is why we include some basic strategies that you must follow to find profitable trades at the right time in this section.

Breakout Trading

One of the most commonly used strategies by traders around the world, breakout trading offers a good profit to those who can time the entry perfectly. In breakout trading, traders wait for a stock's price to break out of a certain range. Most stocks tend to have a fixed range of highs and lows. When a stock breaks out of its upper range, the chances are high that the stock's price is going to increase further. This is the perfect time to buy the stock.

Short-term traders wait for the perfect opportunity and buy a large number of shares in the hope of selling the shares when the prices hit a new high. The breakout trading strategy is best for day traders and swing traders. It is best to enter the market at the start of a new trend so that you can ride the trend from start to end. To accomplish this, you can utilize limit orders so that your trade is executed without you having to monitor the market constantly when a breakout occurs.

Momentum Trading

One of the most utilized strategies of trading is the momentum trading strategy. In momentum trading, the idea is to analyze the movement of stock to understand whether it is rising or dipping. Most readers tend to buy and sell assets based on the strength of the current movements and trends related to stock. It is believed that if the momentum of the current trend is strong, it is most likely to continue in the same direction.

To be an expert at momentum trading, you should focus on the direction of the stock's movement rather than focusing on the top and bottom. If the price of a stock rises in the short term, it will attract traders and investors to buy the stock. This will further increase the price of the stock. If the stock price is decreasing in the short term, traders will try to sell more of the stock. As a result, the price of the stock will fall further downwards.

Range Trading

A popular strategy among short-term traders, range trading, occurs between the lines of resistance and support. Although most long-term traders may find range trading a little ineffective and boring, short-term traders find numerous opportunities to book profit with range trading. Traders take advantage of stocks that usually trade between the two lines. Knowing the range at which a stock usually increases or decreases in price can be utilized profitably.

When the stock is near the bottom range, also known as the line of support, the stock price is likely going to increase. Similarly, at the line of resistance, the range where the stock prices usually start to decrease, traders book profit by setting limit orders. If you want to book profit with range trading, enter the market when the stock is around its known line of support. This will mean that when the stock oscillates upwards in price to reach the line of resistance, you can sell your shares and book a generous profit.

Reversal Trading

This strategy can be utilized perfectly by those traders who can identify when the direction of a stock's movement will change. The change in the movement of a stock is known as a reversal. It is important to note that the reversal of a trend can happen in either direction. To understand it simply, reversal is when the sentiments of the market change and a new trend starts.

When the movement of a stock is downward, a bullish reversal is what indicates the change in direction when the stock starts to move upwards. Most expert traders identify the reversal of a downtrend or uptrend to utilize the change in the market's sentiments to book their profit. Short-term traders can benefit from reversal trading if they can effectively identify and enter the market at the most advantageous point. However, if you are a short-term trader, make sure that the trend is in full reversal before you buy a stock.

The Concept of Time Frames

If you are a beginner in trading, you need to understand the concept of time frames. The amount of time for which a trend lasts in the market is referred to as a time frame. The time frames can range from minutes, hours, days, weeks to years. Most profitable traders utilize time frames to understand the common trends and cycles of the market. In short-term trading, traders utilize primary time frames such as minutes, hours, and days to confirm the movement of the stock and enter the market at the right time. The traders involved in high frequency and day trading benefit the most by analyzing the immediate time frames. However, it is crucial to keep the other time frames in mind to identify trends and patterns that take place in the market.

Being a short-term trader, if you successfully analyze the time frames of a stock correctly, you can greatly increase your chances of booking a profit. You can easily identify contradictions and discord between time frames if you learn to read them successfully.

This will help you improve your timing of buying and selling stock to generate the most profit. Time frames help you to perfect your entries and exits from the market with minimum risk and good returns. By reading time frames successfully and implementing your strategies effectively, you can make confident decisions to accomplish your trading goals.

Analysis Methods Used for Short-Term Trading

To master short-term trading, you must be able to analyze the movements of the market. Every trader has the opportunity to calculate the best timing to buy and sell, along with identifying the best stock. Almost all trading platforms provide you with detailed information that can help you analyze the trend and cycles of the market. This section will discuss the most common analysis methods often used by short-term traders to successfully generate good returns.

Follow the Moving Averages

Simple moving averages are nothing but the average price of a stock over a given period. Moving averages of a stock can be found in its charts. You can find out the moving average of stock for a period of 15, 30, 50, 100, and 200 days. The simple moving averages will help you get an idea of whether a stock is moving upward or downward. To have a profitable trade, it is best to buy shares of a stock that has an upward-inclined moving average. On the other hand, if you are looking to sell a stock, find one that has a declining moving average.

Observe Patterns and Cycles

Observing and identifying patterns and cycles of a market can help you successfully enter and exit with a good amount of profit. It has been observed that from November to April, the market sees the most gains. So, entering a market at the start of November is a good move. Similarly, the months from May to October are generally static in returns as compared to the remaining months of the year. As a short-term trader, you can utilize these cycles and patterns to your advantage. It will also help you perfect your entry and exit timings in the market.

Identify Market Trends

For trade, it is essential to have a sense of identifying market trends. It is best to sell your shares when the market trend seems to be negative. Alternatively, you will profit by buying stocks when the market trend is positive. In addition to this, you should buy very little during negative market trends and sell as little as possible during positive market trends. If you try to trade against the market trend, the chances of having a successful trade decrease dramatically.

Managing the Risks Involved

It's a no-brainer that trading is a risky business. To be a successful trader, you must know how to effectively manage the risks involved in trading. You can only be a good trader when you can maximize your returns with minimum risks. You must be prepared to protect yourself from sudden market reversals. It is best to understand and utilize buy stops and sell stops while trading.

To understand it simply, buy and sell stops are orders to stop buying or selling a stock when the prices reach a high or low. These automatic orders or trades are carried out without you having to constantly monitor the market. So, if you have proper orders in place, you can avoid incurring losses during a downtrend or if the market crashes. According to trading experts, make it a general rule of thumb while short-term trading to set your buy stops and sell stops within 10% of the initial price at which you bought the stock. It is crucial to remember that losses are impossible to avoid in trading. If you manage and minimize your risk, the losses will significantly be less than the gains. And, you'll come out profitable from your short-term trading.

Strategies for Long-Term Trading

When a trader buys and holds an asset for more than a year, it is known as long-term trading. In long-term trading, the traders do not bother themselves with short-term movements in stock prices. Long-term traders are more concerned with long-term trends and the momentum of the market in a larger time frame.

The analysis methods and trading strategies used in long-term trading are similar to short-term trading strategies, except the fact that in long-term trading, the focus is on a larger scale of time. Typically, in long-term trading, traders hold their position for a longer period to gain a larger profit. To help you understand the strategies for long-term trading, here is a bullet list of the most commonly utilized strategies by successful traders.

- **Value Trading** - In this strategy, traders select the stocks that are undervalued and contradictory to the company's earnings potential and long-term fundamentals. Buying a stock when its price is deflated provides an opportunity for traders to earn profits when the stocks increase in value.

- **Benjamin Graham Strategy** - Also known as the intelligent investor strategy, this is when traders select stocks based on high earnings to fixed charge ratio and low debt to equity ratio. In simple terms, the stocks that promise future growth in terms of cash flows and earnings are favored by the traders.
- **Naked Trader Strategy** - In this strategy, traders select the stocks from small and mid-cap companies that have shown profitable earnings and significant growth in the recent past. In addition to this, the value, momentum, P/E ratio, and P/BV ratio play an important role in stock selection.

Methods to Expand and Diversify the Portfolio

Diversifying your trading portfolio is probably the best and easiest way to reduce your risk. By not putting all your eggs in the same basket, you can reduce your chances of incurring huge losses. As a rule of thumb, try to diversify your portfolio so that you can enjoy stable returns with reduced risk. While buying stocks of companies from different sectors is a good start to diversifying your portfolio, here are other methods that you should consider.

- **Spread Your Investments** - Do not put your wealth in similar stocks or sectors. You can also consider investing in commodities and real estate apart from cryptocurrency and mutual funds.

- **Invest in Bonds and Indexes** - Mix up the investments in your portfolio to include fixed-income and index bonds. This will help you stay safe from market uncertainty and volatility.
- **Keep Adding to Your Investments Regularly** - This will help you cut down on your investment risk and build your portfolio over some time by investing the same amount of money over time.

To sum up, let us take a glance at the key takeaways from this chapter. We discovered the various strategies utilized by expert traders for short-term trading. The breakout, momentum, range, and reversal trading strategies are the most effective and commonly used trading strategies to gain significant profits in short-term trading. In addition to this, we discussed the concept of time frames and how they can help you uncover the underlying trends and cycles of the market.

We also discussed the various analysis methods used for short-term trading, such as moving averages, market cycles, and trends. With that said, this chapter also covered the basic strategies used in long-term trading along with some effective ways to minimize the risks involved in trading. And finally, the chapter concluded with some methods to expand and diversify your portfolio to help you gain stable profits with minimum risk.

Chapter 10: Automated Trading

Through technological innovation and the exceptional growth of digital systems, we have revolutionary financial assets such as cryptocurrency. More importantly, we also have systems and methods of trading that were never possible in the past. Cryptocurrency could never have been possible had we not developed computers and digital systems, but through these same technologies, we can also revolutionize the way we trade traditional financial assets.

Just a few short decades ago, stock trading, futures contracts, banking, and every other financial operation was completely manual and required buyers and sellers to come together physically to transact. Digital systems and IT, together with the Internet, have made it possible for us to do business with a person in a different part of the world without ever meeting them or even seeing them.

Just a few years ago, we would never have reached someone even in a different part of the same city as communication methods weren't that advanced. As things changed and communication got better, we could communicate, but business was still slow since there was no way to transact virtually.

Moreover, this improvement in how easy and possible it is for us to connect with people around the globe also opened doors to more investment opportunities.

Today we are not confined to what is locally available. Rather, we can access financial markets all over the world and trade assets that are thousands of miles away from us. Moreover, we never have to interact with these assets ourselves, as everything can be done online.

Automation in Business

In the same way, technology has impacted investments and has had a similar effect on trading and commerce. It has allowed individuals and businesses to trade with other institutions across the globe and given everyone access to a global market.

Consumers can buy from an international market, whereas businesses can sell to a global audience. This means that businesses have more opportunities than ever before while customers have more options to choose from. This globalization of trade makes the market very competitive and gives both buyers and sellers a lot more opportunities.

However, IT and the internet have also greatly affected the way business is carried out, the actual processes used, and how tasks are completed. A good example of the impact of technology in this regard is how commonly businesses create a website and establish their presence online. Regardless of which industry a business is in, businesses all over the world make their websites or at least a social media page to help people find them online. This goes to show how important digital presence has become and how much of a norm it has become to use the internet to find businesses.

Similarly, basic processes like payroll, daily accounting, attendance, and several recurring operations are digital for most businesses. Even small shopkeepers find it much easier to manage inventory through software rather than by managing books.

One of the main benefits of these digital systems is that they can make it possible to automate several processes. At the same time, more complex solutions that use AI may even be able to learn the significance of various tasks and make decisions based on what they have learned. Inventory management systems can automatically place orders to stock when inventory levels reach a certain threshold, just like how payroll systems can automatically generate paychecks using the information provided by the integrated attendance software.

However, even by using simple rules, automation can effectively help people invest and trade commodities. When it comes to cryptocurrencies, several services provide automated investment and trading services that help you minimize loss and maximize returns. Let's look at a few of the most common crypto investment solutions and their unique features.

Automated Investments

While automated trading allows you the freedom to live your life while your investments happen in the background, they don't have to be limited by basic price boundaries that you define, like what you would do with a stock trading service. Rather, automated cryptocurrency trading services give you the flexibility to base your trading protocol on a variety of metrics so you can customize your strategy to meet your requirements.

Some people might prefer to base their trade decision on defined prices, while others might want to pursue a more sophisticated path in which their portfolio automatically rebalances based on proportional values. Let's look at some of the best investment options and how they can work out for you.

Crypto Hopper

Out of many automated crypto trading solutions, Crypto Hopper boasts a complex technical side that is neatly tucked under a user-friendly interface designed to help new traders familiarize themselves with different trading processes. The main advantage of Crypto Hopper is that it allows a lot of the complex analysis to be automated so that the user doesn't have to manually tweak every setting. However, this doesn't mean that the user doesn't need to know what all these metrics mean. It simply makes it easier to manage them.

Crypto Hopper welcomes new users with a free demo to try out the platform. If users choose to use Crypto Hopper full time, they will need to have a minimum deposit of €250 or £250 to begin trading. This platform is home to a wide variety of brokers and offers a plethora of trading signals that traders can use to earn exponential profits. However, user-competence plays a big role in how effectively they can protect themselves from losses and earn profits. Some investors have been able to win fantastic profits on this platform even as beginners by using the different safety systems installed on this platform. One of the best features of this system is the deposit and stop-loss limits which help minimize the risk of your entire portfolio becoming a victim of market volatility.

If you are brand new to crypto trading, it would be a great idea to spend some time on the demo account and get accustomed to how the app works and how the market behaves. Ideally, you should have at least a fundamental understanding of the market and the commodity that you want to trade rather than blindly investing money. This is the only way that you will be able to harness the volatility of the market. Otherwise, you are simply riding waves and hoping you will find land.

Once you are comfortable in the demo account, you can consider putting some real money on the line and moving into live trading. However, as a first-time live trader, it is advisable to use the trading limits when you trade. Extreme volatility in the market is something that no one controls, and even seasoned traders have ruined entire portfolios because they exposed themselves to this threat.

3Commas

The second automated trading platform focused on digital currency assets is 3Commas. Using automated trading bots, this platform aims to minimize the amount of work that traders have to put into their portfolios to earn a profit. With an advanced automated trading process, individuals can make really intricate trades without having to put in a lot of effort. If you are the kind of person who can really narrow down exactly what they want to do in a trade, then you can delegate the entire process to 3Commas, and the platform will handle the actual execution.

However, even with all of its features and services, this is still a platform that can be very beneficial for a beginner as well. 3Commas incorporates a lot of safety features that are vital for new traders, and they also come in handy for more experienced traders. After all, even with years of experience and sizable portfolios, it's in the best interest of even large traders that they keep their losses low. If they can stay away from loss and keep risk at a minimum without too much effort, that's even better.

More than just setting trade limits and creating market orders, 3Commas allows you to automate trailing orders, composite bots, create short sell protocols, and more.

One of the unique features of 3Commas is that it allows you to copy the trading parameters of another trader. This is a fantastic option for people who aren't familiar with the various metrics and don't know how to set up trading parameters properly. You can choose your ideal trader, replicate how they set up their trade protocols, and hopefully enjoy the benefits of their knowledge. It goes without saying that this will work best when you either align yourself with a top trader or look for a trader who shares your interest in a cryptocurrency and style of trading.

Moreover, 3Commas breaks down its services into three membership tiers, starting from roughly $25 per month going all the way up to nearly $80 per month.

MetaTrader

MetaTrader stands out in the financial trading services for a couple of really important reasons.

Firstly, it is one of the few trading interfaces which offers its services completely free of charge. You can buy services that give you additional features, but the basic platform is free for anyone to use. Accessible through the web and mobile, all you need to do is sign up and get started with trading.

The second feature that makes this an incredibly popular choice for a large number of traders is the fact that it is not only restricted to cryptocurrencies. Rather, it allows you to trade a very wide range of financial instruments, whether you are looking to trade forex, futures, stocks, metals, and of course, digital currencies, among many other things. If you are interested in spreading out your investments across a range of financial assets, this is the service that will let you manage everything from a single portal.

A third unique feature that makes MetaTrader a fantastic choice is the option to create custom indicators. MetaTrader comes loaded with 30 standard indicators right out of the box, but it has the option for users to build their own as well. However, this is an advanced feature that will resonate more with seasoned traders with very specific requirements.

Trading Bots

Trading bots are basically specialized pieces of software that assist traders in their trades. Some perform relatively mundane and easy tasks, while others can perform really complicated trades. When using a trading bot, it all boils down to how flexible the software is, how well you can adjust it to suit your preferences, and how effectively it does what it is meant to do.

However, even with the intense functionality that they offer, these are options that aren't very beginner-friendly for the simple reason that it takes quite a lot of expertise and an in-depth understanding to get them to work right. It's like managing a high-performance athlete: they are amazing physical specimens, but it requires a solid coach to really direct their efforts and make them profitable in one specific area.

Similarly, while it is not very complicated to get a trading bot, it can be difficult for a beginner to identify the exact kind that they need and then be able to properly set it up to do what they want it to do. However, if you know or are willing to learn how to manage a trading bot, they are extremely powerful pieces of software that can be incredible trading partners.

With the ability to watch and learn the market, predict risk, and do many other things, having the right trading bot is definitely a very valuable addition to any trading team.

Python Programming

Python is arguably one of the most favorite languages with data scientists today. In fact, data scientists, crypto-coders, and traders are making use of this modern language as it is a great tool for anyone working with data. Not only does it offer incredible functionality and versatility in the things that can be done within, but it is relatively easy to learn and has a wide application.

Whether you are looking to mine coins, create a custom market monitoring software, or even develop your very own cryptocurrency, you can achieve all your goals through Python.

One of the main attractions for people to work with Python is the fact that it does not require compilation. Unlike other languages such as C++, which require a piece of code to be compiled before machines can understand it, Python can be run directly as it is, which reduces a very time-consuming process in the life of a coder.

Crypto Exchanges

Just like traditional stock exchanges, crypto exchanges serve as a platform where sellers and buyers of different cryptocurrencies can come together to trade their assets. Crypto exchanges share many of the traits of traditional exchanges in how they are structured and how they perform. However, there are some broad differences in the main types of cryptocurrencies which we will discuss below.

Centralized

Centralized exchanges are generally governed by a group of companies or a single company that overlooks the exchange's performance and offers its services to users that are trading through it. As these exchanges rely on a governing body for direction, they have tighter regulations and legislation that both traders and cryptocurrencies have to adhere to and are considered more secure than other exchanges.

Moreover, these exchanges also allow for traders to trade from crypto-to-crypto or from fiat currency to crypto. Due to their highly secure infrastructure and relatively easy access, they are popular with new traders and offer a better user experience than other options. The fact that these governing bodies also act as custodians of funds makes these exchanges a lot more reliable since every part of the trade process is to quite an extent in the control of these governing bodies.

Decentralized

As the name suggests, these exchanges move away from the regulated structure of the centralized exchange and place a greater emphasis on enabling traders to connect with each other directly, which is why they are also sometimes referred to as peer-to-peer exchanges. As the intervention of a governing body is reduced, many people think that these exchanges are not reliable and less secure.

Though, on the upside, these exchanges offer a lot more freedom, privacy, and potentially a higher scope of earning for traders. Moreover, these decentralized exchanges deal exclusively in crypto-to-crypto trades, so it's not possible to enter with fiat currency, let alone trade with it. One of the major downsides to working on a decentralized exchange is that investors often find it difficult to offload a currency when they want to sell and buy a currency when they want to invest because they have relatively low liquidity.

Hybrid

Hybrid exchanges aim to provide traders with the benefits of the two previously mentioned exchanges while trying to eliminate the downsides of both of them, so the client gets the best of both worlds.

By using smart contracts, hybrid exchanges try to improve their security and reliability, and without a governing body, they try to give traders a bit more room and a bit more freedom than centralized exchanges.

Chapter 11: Keeping Your Investments Safe

Now that you've learned everything you need about cryptocurrencies, including different types, trading platforms, and strategies, there's one last important aspect to bear in mind - perhaps the most pressing for beginners like yourself. Given the risky nature of cryptocurrency investments, you must be wondering how you will keep your investments safe, especially when there is regular news about horrifying cases of scams, enough to make you want to drop the whole idea altogether. In this chapter, you will learn about the different types of scams, how to spot them, and how to deal with them.

You will also get to understand the basics of safe cryptocurrency investing to make sure you don't fall victim to those malicious attempts. This is a critical stage of your cryptocurrency learning, so make sure you have a pen and paper handy and start taking notes:

Most Common Scamming Methods

Over the years, cryptocurrency scamming methods have become more sophisticated and much harder to detect. However, through keen observation, you can identify a certain pattern to confirm if/when you're being targeted. Below you will find more information about the most common scamming methods, the risks they entail, and how to protect yourself against each.

Classic Scams

Scams that fall under this category are the ones that have been around for quite some time yet, somehow are still working, especially with newbie traders. Random emails from questionable addresses and strange phone calls are among the top classic scamming techniques that threaten traders and put their investments at risk. They're very straightforward and sometimes even naïve. However, you'd be surprised how many people tend to forget all about common sense when there's money involved. Some of the typical scenarios involve a request from the scammer to immediately transfer X amount of money to avoid being taxed for your cryptocurrency winnings.

Your lack of experience and ignorance of the investment process will cause such panic at the possibility of being incriminated that you'd be willing to respond without pausing to consider if this even makes sense. Here's how you can protect yourself against classic scams:

- **Always Be Suspicious**

Given the modest concept behind classic scams, there really isn't much to do except for relying on your good judgment when receiving any suspicious correspondences. Look into the email address and request some kind of verification to ensure that the sender/caller is who they claim to be. If you're ever asked to make any financial transactions, there should be an official payment slip from an authorized entity. You can also take advantage of the hundreds of online forums and cryptocurrency platforms where you can post an inquiry about any fishy requests you receive. More experienced traders will definitely share some valuable insights and tips on how you should respond and what you need to do for future reference.

Phishing

Phishing is one of the most common social engineering scams that have to do with stealing sensitive data. The scammer usually sends an email posing as your cryptocurrency platform or wallet provider containing a coded link. Once opened, you're directed to an illegitimate website where the attacker gets access to your personal information, online accounts' passwords, and credit card details. Basically, any information that can be linked back to you could be within their reach in a matter of seconds. With phishing, your trading details, especially your wallet keys, are susceptible to confiscation, which means that the entire wallet you've spent months or maybe years building could be at risk. For less-experienced individuals, phishing could be difficult to detect. However, some of the precautionary measures that you can apply are:

- **Don't Open Any Links**

Unless you're one hundred percent sure that the links you receive in an email are legitimate, you should never open them. This applies to messages you receive on any platform as there's a chance your email address is hacked, and the attacker has access to all of your online accounts.

- **Verify the URL of the Website**

Only encrypted websites that start with HTTPS are considered genuine and safe for you to visit. If you receive an email with a link connecting you to an unencrypted website, this is your cue to run as fast as you can. Changing your passwords after similar incidents wouldn't be an overreaction. It's actually a good way to ensure that your funds are safe and sound. Besides checking the encryption, you can also call up the claimed sender, whether it's your bank or your cryptocurrency platform, and ask for their confirmation about the email and the attached link. When it comes to ensuring the security of your investments, there's no such thing as too much.

- **Stay Up-To-Date with Latest Phishing Techniques**

It's your responsibility to protect yourself against phishing scams. Your wallet provider, your bank, or any other entity cannot be blamed for your negligence. Nowadays, there is a myriad of sources that you can rely on to stay updated about the latest phishing techniques that are trending worldwide. Make sure you join the conversations that have to do with cryptocurrency trading risks to have a clear idea about the right course of action post-scam.

Illegitimate Cryptocurrency Exchanges

Beware of the cryptocurrency deals that might seem too good because they're fake more often than not. Transactions that offer you special perks like tempting initial depositing bonuses or special trading schemes specifically designed for your needs should make you wary. The scammers might pay you back part of the promised funds, however not for long. It's all part of the play until they can acquire as much of your funds as possible. Unfortunately, these scams are not very easy to spot since sometimes public figures and social media influencers promote them. This makes unsuspecting traders like yourself more willing to trust the promoted transaction and putting your funds at risk.

- **Only Trade in Trusted Exchanges**

As a general rule, regardless of how attractive an exchange seems to be, unless it's popular and common among traders, don't fall for it. Be very skeptical and don't save any efforts in researching and verifying the exchange. Given the extent of the associated risk, you will judge it as a small price to pay if you get to keep your funds secure and out of the reach of skilled scammers.

- **Look for Reviews from Other Users**

Sometimes the best way to confirm that an exchange is indeed legitimate is to research reviews from other users. Make it a point to only go with exchanges that seem to be in high demand, and other users are sharing positive feedback about their experiences.

- **Refrain from Sharing Personal Data**

And not only with cryptocurrency platforms. As a general rule, you shouldn't feel forced to disclose your personal information or passwords on any platform. Nor should you make any financial deposits unless you understand where exactly your money is going and how it will be used.

Initial Coin Offering (ICO) Scams

Companies - usually startups - issue a new cryptocurrency as a way to raise funds from interested investors. This offers scammers a great opportunity to take advantage of the situation, either through creating a completely fake currency from the start or redirecting the public traffic toward a fraudulent website. In both cases, the scammers are using the ICO as a cover for their malicious attacks.

- **Research the ICO Thoroughly**

With the abundant stories about people who became rich almost overnight after having invested in the ICO of one of the major cryptocurrencies, it's easy to understand why and how one would fall for the fake ones. After all, the whole idea of becoming a trader is to make money. So, when a seemingly lucrative chance comes your way to become one of the early investors promising attractive returns, you should pay attention but tread with caution. Use governmental resources that offer valuable tips about telling a legitimate ICO from a fake one. Furthermore, you should do your own due diligence to find out who's behind this ICO, what are the specifics of the new cryptocurrency, and why it is being released in the first place. In other words, you should play detective and not give in unless you have all the assurances you need to believe that an ICO is, in fact, a real one.

- **Find Out if the Entity Behind the ICO Is Compliant with the Law**

Even though this seems like reasonable advice, inexperienced traders often ignore it in their excitement about becoming early investors. Cryptocurrency investments are governed by the Securities and Exchange Committee (SEC) in most countries. However, unlike regular securities, in cryptocurrency markets, investors have little to no protection.

This makes them more susceptible to fraudulent deals and fake investment opportunities. In the case of a new ICO, the SEC has a set of laws and regulations to be followed and fulfilled before they could be approved. When an ICO opportunity comes your way, you should confirm compliance with governmental decrees before you make any decision about whether or not you should partake.

Phone-Porting Scams

The idea behind phone-porting scams is very basic. Scammers target your cellphone's SIM card to gain access to your crypto wallet, reset the password and take over your account. In a matter of a few seconds, you could lose it all. Scammers can take hold of your cell phone in multiple ways. Bribing your phone carrier or hacking your phone to steal your personal information data are only a few of the ways you could be under the threat of SIM scammers.

- **Don't Link Your Phone to Your Crypto Wallet**

A simple and easy way to protect yourself against phone-porting scams is to avoid linking your phone to your crypto wallet. That's fairly easy in theory. However, it's quite the hassle in practice because, like most people, you probably rely on your phone for everything, including managing your crypto wallet and trading. But, the risk of getting scammed and losing your funds is too big to take any chances.

- **Use an Authentication App**

To authenticate your account and avoid phone-porting, replace your phone authentication with one of the specialized authentication apps. Available on common app stores, you can find a selection of authentication apps that come with a variety of security features to ensure your data protection. However, before you download any random authentication app, you should make sure that it actually does what it claims to do. Search other users' reviews and look into the listed features before you invest in one of the paid-for apps.

Giveaways Scam

Here, the scammer takes over one of the public figure's accounts to announce fake cryptocurrency giveaways in exchange for an initial deposit on your side. The scammer makes it look like their accounts are real and even verified on social media platforms to call potential victims into immediate action. As a beginner, coming across similar attractive offers could be hard to resist, especially if it looks legitimate and is sponsored by popular celebrities or other "trusted" parties. Once you fall for it and decide to pay the asking price to participate in the giveaway, the scammer takes your money and disappears into thin air.

- **Use a Blockchain Explorer**

A blockchain explorer is software that keeps track of all cryptocurrency transactions and can provide you with real-time information about the movements in the blockchain network. This should show you the inflow versus the outflow on the provided blockchain address. If you notice that the outflow is insignificant in comparison, then it's probably a scam, and you don't need to dig any further.

- **Be Suspicious When a Celebrity is Claimed to be Doing a Giveaway**

Assuming that celebrities have more awareness than to get involved in these shady deals, any time you see a giveaway being hyped about, don't buy into it. Practice caution and try to read between the lines. If you look closely, you'll almost always find a spelling mistake that gives the scam away.

Pyramid Scams

Also known as high-return scams, pyramid schemes have been around for a long time, way before cryptocurrencies. This is when the scammer convinces you to deposit a pay-out to get under his network/pyramid and make unusually high returns. The scammer is already working in parallel with other unsuspecting traders, promising them the same. What happens next is that the scammer pays you from other investors' pay-out funds- to make you believe in the legitimacy of the process and that it's actually working. Before you know it, the scammer disappears with the money, and you and others are left with only the regret of getting involved in the first place.

- **Keep in Mind that Unrealistic Returns are Almost Always a Scam**

When you're promised exaggerated returns, you should always get suspicious. Especially if it's fairly easy to find out the average returns on cryptocurrency investments.

- **Don't Get into a Transaction Where You're Asked to Bring In Other Investors**

As mentioned above, from your experience with the old-school pyramid schemes, if a cryptocurrency exchange comes conditional on bringing in other investors, simply run the other way! Authentic cryptocurrency platforms might offer you some sort of bonus for bringing in a new investor on board, but it's never conditional on accepting your buy-in.

The above scams are among the latest, most common scams that you need to be aware of as a beginner in the world of cryptocurrency. In addition to the mentioned tips on how to avoid falling for each, you'd be pleased to know that you can actually play an active role in maintaining the security of the cryptocurrency network through "Staking Crypto".

What Is Staking Crypto?

In an attempt to make the cryptocurrency network even more self-sufficient, this process entails having investor's support in securing and sustaining the network in exchange for financial compensation. As an active member, this should be an interesting opportunity for you to ensure that your and other investors' investments are protected from scammers.

How Does Staking Crypto Work?

Interested traders carry out a process called Proof of Staking (POS). This happens as traders put away some tokens to validate all of the transactions that take place through the blockchain. In addition to the enhanced security, one of the main benefits of POS is saving otherwise wasted mining efforts to validate each new transaction.

Risks of Staking

Despite its benefits, validators involved in staking crypto are burdened with a set of risks, including:

- **Long Staking Duration**: As a staker, you might be asked to lock up your tokens for a pre-specified duration. If, at any point, the value of your assets drops and you can't reach them to sell, this will impact the value of your aggregate wallet. However, there is a work-around where you avoid stackable assets that come with long staking durations.
- **Market Fluctuations:** The asset you choose to put up for staking could bear a drop-in value far bigger than what you're gaining in staking returns. Although hard to predict, you can try to be more assertive when choosing which assets to stake.
- **Associated Validating Costs:** As a validator, you will need to invest in hardware and electricity to run the validator node. So, you should always make sure to keep your costs below your staking-returns margins to remain profitable.

This chapter should help you trade safely as you venture into the vast world of cryptocurrencies. Make sure you understand the implications of your investing decisions and the amount of risk you're bearing at all times.

Conclusion

This comprehensive book highlighted various concepts about cryptocurrency that every beginner should know. As a recap, a cryptocurrency is also known as a digital currency that you can use to buy various goods and services. The currency utilizes an online ledger, and it consists of strong cryptography that is designed to secure all online transactions. Cryptocurrency is unregulated, unlike fiat currencies that central banks in different countries control. In short, a cryptocurrency is a universal currency that can be used across borders without any issues in places where it is accepted.

The other point of interest with these unregulated currencies is that they can be traded for profit, and speculators at times can drive prices upwards. Cryptocurrency trading can be highly profitable, but like any other online trade, there are different things that you should know. The terminology used in cryptocurrency trading can sound intimidating, but you must understand it to succeed in your trade.

As you have observed in this book, there is no way you can talk of cryptocurrency trading without mentioning the term blockchain. A blockchain is a special form of database which stores data in blocks, and these are chained together. All new data is stored in a fresh block, and the blocks are chained together in chronological order. The primary purpose of a blockchain is that it is used as a ledger for transactions. No single person has control of the unregulated cryptocurrency. The other crucial aspect of decentralized blockchains is that they are immutable, meaning that they cannot be reversed once the data is entered.

Another essential component of cryptocurrency that you should know is crypto mining. Apart from trading cryptocurrency, you can also earn it through the mining process, which involves verifying transactions between different users. The process involves validating data blocks which helps to add transaction records to the blockchain public ledger. The miners get a reward in the form of cryptocurrency for the work performed.

This process of crypto mining also involves the creation of new cryptocurrencies through solving puzzles or cryptographic equations using computers. The introduction of new coins in the supply circulation is one of the key factors that allow different cryptocurrencies to work as a decentralized network.

In this book, you have also learned that there are different types of cryptocurrencies, and more than 10,000 are traded publicly. More cryptocurrencies continue to emerge, but the popular ones include Bitcoin, Ethereum, Binance Coin, Tether, Cardano, Polkadot, Ripple, Litecoin, Chainlink, and Stellar. Before you start trading in cryptocurrency, you should choose the right crypto. You need to understand its benefits over other cryptocurrencies.

You also need to understand the vital step of choosing the crypto wallet that you will use for all your transactions. As you have noted in this book, there are different types of crypto wallets: mobile wallets, online wallets, block, desktop wallets, paper wallets, loaf wallets, and hardware wallets. It is vital to understand how to choose a wallet considering elements like fees and security. Additionally, you also need to understand how to choose the best trading platforms. The platform that you select will play a pivotal role in determining the success of your trade. Evaluate different platforms and outline their pros and cons.

Understanding technical analysis is another important aspect of cryptocurrency trading. You should know the basics of technical analysis, reading different types of charts, and the importance of the psychology of the trader. You should not just wake up and decide to invest in cryptocurrency. There are different reasons why you can consider cryptocurrency mining or trading. Some people turn to cryptocurrency trading because it is flexible, and it gives them financial freedom. Unlike fiat currency that is centralized and controlled by a central government, cryptocurrency is decentralized. The area of cryptocurrency mining is significantly gaining popularity with many investors.

However, it is also attracting cyber criminals who are bent on trying their luck. Therefore, you should know the risks associated with cryptocurrency trading, like scams. Market volatility is another major risk that you should be aware of. Crypto trading is fundamentally based on speculative buying where the buyers anticipate that the price will spike, which will help them generate more profits.

To succeed in your trade, you should know different strategies. For instance, short-term trading and long-term trading strategies are all suitable for different time frames. With the right knowledge, you can choose trading methods that help you expand and diversify your portfolio.

Automated trading is designed for both beginners and established traders. As you have observed above, you can cut losses with limited orders that allow you to trade with money that you are prepared to lose. More importantly, you have learned the basic measures that you can take to keep your investment safe. You should be wary of scams, red flags, and unrealistic returns. Other offers are just too good to be true.

References

Lambert, C. (2019, September 30). Cryptocurrency Basics: A Beginner's Guide (2021 Update). Retrieved from Wealthfit.com website: https://wealthfit.com/articles/cryptocurrency-basics/

More, R. (2018, January 11). What is cryptocurrency? Beginners guide to digital cash - NerdWallet. Retrieved from Nerdwallet.com website: https://www.nerdwallet.com/article/investing/cryptocurrency-7-things-to-know

Sumner, A. (2021, January 12). Cryptocurrency is an electronic, private type of money - here's how it works and how you can invest in it. Retrieved from Business Insider India website: https://www.businessinsider.in/stock-market/news/cryptocurrency-is-an-electronic-private-type-of-money-heres-how-it-works-and-how-you-can-invest-in-it/articleshow/80238624.cms

Conway, L. (2021, June 1). Blockchain Explained. Retrieved from Investopedia.com website: https://www.investopedia.com/terms/b/blockchain.asp

What is blockchain technology? How does it work? (n.d.). Retrieved from Builtin.com website: https://builtin.com/blockchain

More, R. (2018a, January 11). What is cryptocurrency? Beginners guide to digital cash - NerdWallet. Retrieved from Nerdwallet.com website: https://www.nerdwallet.com/article/investing/cryptocurrency-7-things-to-know

Binance Academy. (2018, December 6). What is cryptocurrency mining? Retrieved from Binance.com website: https://academy.binance.com/en/articles/what-is-cryptocurrency-mining

Crane, C. (2020, October 16). What is crypto mining? How cryptocurrency mining works. Retrieved from Sectigostore.com website: https://sectigostore.com/blog/what-is-crypto-mining-how-cryptocurrency-mining-works/

(Aguirre, 2018) Aguirre, F. G. (2018, May 21). Why are there so many cryptocurrencies? Retrieved from Bobsguide.com website: https://www.bobsguide.com/articles/why-are-there-so-many-cryptocurrencies/

(Conway, 2021) Conway, L. (2021, June 21). Cardano (ADA). Retrieved from Investopedia.com website: https://www.investopedia.com/cardano-definition-4683961

(Frankenfield, 2021) Frankenfield, J. (2021, May 19). Binance Coin (BNB). Retrieved from Investopedia.com website: https://www.investopedia.com/terms/b/binance-coin-bnb.asp

("No title," n.d.) No title. (n.d.). Forbes Magazine. Retrieved from https://www.forbes.com/advisor/investing/what-is-bitcoin/

("No title," n.d.) No title. (n.d.). Forbes Magazine. Retrieved from https://www.forbes.com/advisor/investing/what-is-ethereum-ether/

("No title," n.d.) No title. (n.d.). Forbes Magazine. Retrieved from https://www.investopedia.com/articles/investing/040515/what-litecoin-and-how-does-it-work.asp

(Ong, 2021) Ong, J. Y. (2021, June 6). How does Tether (USDT) work, and why is it so controversial? Retrieved from Makeuseof.com website: https://www.makeuseof.com/how-does-tether-usdt-work-and-why-is-it-so-controversial/

(Polkadot, 2020) Polkadot. (2020, May 14). What is Polkadot? A Brief Introduction. Retrieved from Polkadot.network website: https://polkadot.network/what-is-polkadot-a-brief-introduction/

(Sharma, 2021) Sharma, R. (2021, April 6). What is stellar blockchain? Retrieved from Investopedia.com website: https://www.investopedia.com/news/what-stellar/

("What is Chainlink? Oracles, nodes and LINK tokens," n.d.) What is Chainlink? Oracles, nodes and LINK tokens. (n.d.). Retrieved from Gemini.com website: https://www.gemini.com/cryptopedia/what-is-chainlink-and-how-does-it-work

A complete guide to pick your cryptocurrency wallet (in 2021). (2018, December 18). Retrieved from Coinzilla.com website: https://academy.coinzilla.com/cryptocurrency-wallet-guide/

LoafWallet is the first server-free litecoin wallet for iOS. (2016, August 2). Retrieved from Bitcoinist.com website: https://bitcoinist.com/loafwallet-server-free-litecoin-wallet/

Michael. (2018, March 13). 11 things to consider before you choose a crypto wallet, exchange, or ICO. Retrieved from Hobowithalaptop.com website: https://hobowithalaptop.com/can-you-trust-your-crypto

Murillo, K. (2021, June 23). 5 cryptocurrency wallets to keep your digital coins safe. Retrieved from Masterdc.com website: https://www.masterdc.com/blog/best-cryptocurrency-wallets/

(N.d.). Retrieved from Coinsutra.com website: https://coinsutra.com/types-of-crypto-wallets/amp/

Best Bitcoin Exchange Staff. (2019, January 22). Kraken.com Review 2021 – Scam or Not? Retrieved from Bestbitcoinexchange.net website: https://www.bestbitcoinexchange.net/en/kraken-com/

Fankhauser, D. (2021, January 13). Cash App review (updated 2021): Pros, cons and how it compares. Retrieved from Bitcompare.net website: https://bitcompare.net/reviews/cash-app

Horvath, S. (2021a, May 12). TradeStation review. Retrieved from Benzinga.com website: https://www.benzinga.com/money/tradestation-review/

Horvath, S. (2021b, June 21). Uphold review. Retrieved from Benzinga.com website: https://www.benzinga.com/money/uphold-review/

Reinkensmeyer, B., & Hatzakis, S. (2021, January 18). Best online brokers for bitcoin trading. Retrieved from Stockbrokers.com website: https://www.stockbrokers.com/guides/best-crypto-exchanges-bitcoin-trading

Hayes, A. (2021, May 19). Introduction to technical analysis price patterns. Retrieved from Investopedia.com website: https://www.investopedia.com/articles/technical/112601.asp

Technical analysis for bitcoin and other crypto. (n.d.). Retrieved from Gemini.com website: https://www.gemini.com/cryptopedia/technical-analysis-bitcoin-and-crypto

6 reasons to invest and trade in cryptocurrency in 2020. (2019, December 4). Retrieved from Digitalistmag.com website: https://www.digitalistmag.com/digital-economy/2019/12/04/6-reasons-to-invest-trade-in-cryptocurrency-in-2020-06201759/

Brockman, K. (2021, May 12). 2 reasons to invest in cryptocurrency -- and 3 reasons not to. Retrieved from The Motley Fool website: https://www.fool.com/investing/2021/05/12/2-reasons-to-invest-in-cryptocurrency-and-3-reason/

Finextra. (2021, May 12). Should you invest in cryptocurrencies right now? Retrieved from Finextra.com website: https://www.finextra.com/blogposting/20295/should-you-invest-in-cryptocurrencies-right-now

Analyst, I. G. (2019, December 17). Short-term trading strategies for beginners. Retrieved from IG website: https://www.ig.com/en/trading-strategies/short-term-trading-strategies-for-beginners-191217.amp

CapitalVia. (2020, July 1). The Best Strategies for long term investments (Guide for Beginners). Retrieved from Capitalvia.com website: https://www.capitalvia.com/blog/long-term-investments-strategies-for-beginners

Fundora, J. (2021, May 19). Multiple time frames can multiply returns. Retrieved from Investopedia.com website: https://www.investopedia.com/articles/trading/07/timeframes.asp

Palmer, B. (2021, June 3). 5 tips for diversifying your portfolio. Retrieved from Investopedia.com website: https://www.investopedia.com/articles/03/072303.asp

Seabury, C. (2021, May 19). Mastering short-term trading. Retrieved from Investopedia.com website: https://www.investopedia.com/articles/trading/09/short-term-trading.asp

Finextra. (2021, April 21). Everything you need to know about Crypto Trading Bots. Retrieved from Finextra.com website: https://www.finextra.com/blogposting/20185/everything-you-need-to-know-about-crypto-trading-bots

(N.d.). Retrieved from Coininsider.com website: https://www.coininsider.com/crypto-hopper-review/

8 types of cryptocurrency scams & Bitcoin frauds to watch out for. (2021, May 27). Retrieved from Moneycrashers.com website: https://www.moneycrashers.com/types-cryptocurrency-scams/

Falk, T. (2017, November 22). 10 common Bitcoin scams (and how to avoid them). Retrieved from Finder.com website: https://www.finder.com/bitcoin-scams

Kaspersky. (2021, January 13). 4 common cryptocurrency scams and how to avoid them. Retrieved from Kaspersky.com website: https://www.kaspersky.com/resource-center/definitions/cryptocurrency-scams

Liebkind, J. (2021, May 20). Beware of these five bitcoin scams. Retrieved from Investopedia.com website: https://www.investopedia.com/articles/forex/042315/beware-these-five-bitcoin-scams.asp

Liquid. (n.d.). How to avoid falling victim to common cryptocurrency scams. Retrieved from Liquid.com website: https://blog.liquid.com/how-to-avoid-scam-in-crypto

No title. (n.d.). Retrieved from Capital.com website: https://capital.com/what-is-staking-in-crypto-a-closer-look-at-the-rise-of-pos

SEC.gov. (2017, December 11). Retrieved from Sec.gov website: https://www.sec.gov/news/public-statement/statement-clayton-2017-12-11

Top 7 risks of staking crypto. (n.d.). Retrieved from Trustwallet.com website: https://trustwallet.com/blog/top-7-risks-of-staking-crypto